The Crafty Reader

The Crafty Reader

Robert Scholes

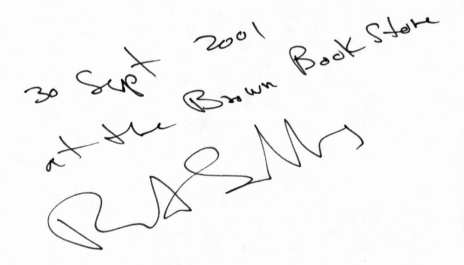

30 Sept 2001
at the Brown Book Store

Yale University Press   New Haven and London

Designed by Sonia Shannon.
Set in Cochin type by The Composing Room
of Michigan, Inc., Grand Rapids, Michigan.
Printed in the United States of America by
R. R. Donnelley & Sons, Harrisonburg, Virginia.

Library of Congress Cataloging-in-Publication Data
Scholes, Robert E.
    The crafty reader / Robert Scholes
        p. cm.
Includes bibliographical references (p.) and index.
    ISBN 0-300-09015-3 (alk. paper)
    1. English literature — History and criticism —
Theory, etc.   2. American literature — History and
criticism — Theory, etc.   3. Literature — Appreciation.
4. Reader-response criticism.   5. Books and reading.
6. Literary form.   I. Title.
    PR21.S36   2001
    028 — dc21   00-013134
A catalogue record for this book is available from the
British Library.

The paper in this book meets the guidelines for
permanence and durability of the Committee on
Production Guidelines for Book Longevity of the
Council on Library Resources.

10 9 8 7 6 5 4 3 2 1

To David Fuchs, my roommate for those bright college years, my friend for half a century and more. The good conversation has never stopped. May it go on a while longer.

Contents

Acknowledgments

Too many colleagues and students at Brown University have reacted to the ideas in this book for me to do a proper job of recognizing their contributions, but I will take a stab at noticing some of them. In particular the undergraduate and graduate students in the following courses helped me develop and refine my thinking: "A Low Dishonest Decade," "The Rise of the Private Eye," and "The Monstrous Personal Chronicle." I must also thank my graduate students in the Program in Literary Theory at the University of Lisbon for saving me from errors in the one essay in this book that they read—and for other kindnesses as well. Janet Sharistanian and her colleagues at the University of Kansas forced me to sharpen and develop what became the first chapter of this book. The opportunities given me by the National Council of Teachers of English to speak to high school and college English teachers were extremely important, as were the responses I received on those occasions. Khachig Tölölyan of Wesleyan University graciously shared his vast learning with me. Finally, my colleague Sean Latham made some important suggestions for revisions to the completed first draft. And Gerald Graff gave the manuscript a bracing critical reading. All these people did their best. Any problems that remain are all my own.

For permission to use images by Norman Rockwell in this book I am grateful to Tom Rockwell and the Norman Rockwell Family Trust. I am also grateful to Scotty Ingram for helping me obtain prints of these images and for sharing his unique knowledge of Norman Rockwell with me.

Introduction

Reading as a Craft

This man, this artisan, had seventeen waistcoats to arrange
in his window, with as many sets of cufflinks and neckties
surrounding them. He spent about eleven minutes on each:
we timed him. We left, tired out, after the sixth item. We
had been there for *one hour* in front of that man, who would
come out to see the effect after having adjusted these things
one millimeter. Each time he came out he was so absorbed
that he did not see us. With the dexterity of a fitter, he
arranged his spectacle, brow wrinkled, eyes fixed, as if his
whole future life depended on it. When I think of the care-
lessness and lack of discipline in the work of certain artists,
well-known painters, whose pictures are sold for so much
money, we should deeply admire this *worthy craftsman,* forg-
ing his own work with difficulty and conscientiousness,
which is more valuable than those expensive canvases;
they are going to disappear, but he will have to renew his
work in a few days with the same care and the same keenness. Men like this, such artisans, have a concept of art —
one closely tied to commercial purposes, but one that is a
plastic achievement of a new order and the equivalent of
existing artistic manifestations, whatever they may be.

Fernand Léger

This craftsmanship, storytelling, was actually regarded as a craft by Leskov himself. "Writing," he says in one of his letters, "is to me no liberal art but a craft." . . . In fact one can go on and ask oneself whether the relationship of the storyteller to his material, human life, is not in itself a craftsman's relationship, whether it is not his very task to fashion the raw material of experience, his own and that of others, in a solid, useful, and unique way.

Walter Benjamin

Fernand Léger, writing in 1924, and Walter Benjamin, in 1936, offer us two ways into the complex relationship between art and craft. For Benjamin craft was a quality to be found in the work of a nineteenth-century storyteller like Nikolai Leskov, who drew consciously upon the methods and materials of an earlier age. The verbal arts, Benjamin felt, were suffering in an age dominated by "information," rootless factoids that threatened both the earlier modes of "storytelling" (epic and tale) and also the forms that had replaced them — the novel and the short story. His brilliant essay "The Storyteller," from which my second epigraph is taken, is a nostalgic celebration of Leskov and the "incomparable aura about the storyteller" (109). Léger, on the other hand (in the first epigraph), saw in the efforts of a window dresser a craftsmanship that called into question the careless work of some contemporary artists.

I do not think that the German critic and the French painter are actually very far apart here on the value of craftsmanship. Both admired it and were concerned about its survival in an era dominated by "commercial purposes" and "information." And both were keenly aware of the way that art and craft might be inimical to each other. But Benjamin saw craft as something inevitably doomed in an age of information and mechanical reproduction, while Léger found it still alive in both mechanical work and commodity culture. Léger, of course, in his own work with paint, metal, ceramics, and film, tried to maintain that craftsman's ethos — tried and largely succeeded, I would say, making him one of the most admirable of the modernists. Different as their views of the matter may be, however, both writers valued what is solid, useful, and conscientious in craft (their adjectives), though they found it in different places. They were thinking of things from the producer's point of view rather than the consumer's, but their discussions imply a notion of consumption, a solid and conscientious way of reading verbal and visual texts that I wish to call — for reasons that should be apparent already — "crafty." In this book, then, I shall be proposing that we all try to become crafty readers: that we learn to read with the care and keenness displayed by Léger's window dresser, and that we also learn to take seriously the work of such crafty artisans as Edna Millay, Norman Rockwell, Raymond Chandler, and J. K. Rowling.

One becomes a crafty reader by learning the craft of reading. I believe that it is in our interest as individuals to become crafty readers, and in the interest of the nation to educate citizens in the craft of reading. The craft, not the art. Art is high, craft is low. Art is unique; it can't be taught. Craft is common; it can be learned. There are virtuoso readers, who produce readings that are breathtakingly original, but the more original these readers become, the less they remain readers. Their readings become new works, writings, if you will, for which the originals were only pretexts, and those who create them become authors. I am not interested in producing such readings myself, nor do I believe that anyone can teach others to produce them. What can be studied, learned, and taught is the craft of reading. This book is about that craft. It is an attempt to explain and embody ways of reading that anyone can learn. It is not, however, a textbook on the craft of reading. I would not wish to suggest that reading this book will turn anyone into a crafty reader. I am hoping, merely, to persuade my readers of the existence of such a craft, and to show how it differs from some other ways of reading, such as that advocated by the New Critics or that which I call "fundamentalist." I also hope to show how this approach to reading will allow us to bring forward for serious consideration certain crafty texts that are now largely outside the boundaries of literary study. To this end I shall spend a good deal of time talking about the ways in which readers "situate" texts, and about the role of literary "genres" in the process of situation.

What is the craft of reading? As with any craft, reading depends on the use of certain tools, handled with skill. But the tools of reading are not simply there, like a hammer or a chisel; they must be acquired, through practice. The essays in this book are all attempts to demonstrate how some of these tools work, and to show how they may be acquired. I have arranged them in an order that makes sense to me, but they need not be read in that order. They will, I hope, support one another, regardless of the order in which they are read. In writing them I have been trying to sharpen my own command of the craft of reading — to become a craftier reader — and to make the practice of the craft — the tricks of the trade, so to speak — more open to use by those who, like myself, still hope to improve as readers. I am well aware that reading now extends beyond the written word into various other kinds of verbal and visual texts, but I have not tried to push too far into those domains, being uncertain whether my own craft would justify this.

New media, in any case, do not exactly replace or eliminate old ones. They take their places in a world of communication; they require realignments of that world; they borrow from the older ways of composing texts; and they change — often enrich — the older forms themselves. The arrival of new media often generates a gap between accepted or "high" texts and those new texts regarded with suspicion or simply labeled "low." The popular drama in Shakespeare's time was regarded as low and only gradually achieved high status. Following a similar trajectory, the novel began as a low form and was gradually elevated to the level of literary art. More recently, we find film following the same pattern. But the rise of so many new media, so recently, has threatened to leave us with a deep gap between what is thought of as "high" art or literature, on the one hand, and "mass" or "popular" culture, on the other. Without rejecting the notion that some texts are indeed better than others (for some purposes), I will assert here, and maintain throughout this book, that valuable texts are to be found in all media, and in many genres within those media. I will also assume that we make a mistake if we equate the difficult and the obscure with the valuable — a mistake frequently made, especially by teachers and professors of literature. But now it is time for me to start making my own mistakes. I hope you will follow me and pick me up if I stumble.

The Crafty Reader

Reading Poetry

A Lost Craft

There is a word, a "name of fear," which rouses terror in the heart of the vast educated majority of the English-speaking race. The most valiant will fly at the mere utterance of that word. The most broad-minded will put their backs up against it. The most rash will not dare affront it. I myself have seen it empty buildings that had been full; and I know that it will scatter a crowd more quickly than a hose-pipe, hornets, or the rumour of plague. Even to murmur it is to incur solitude, probably disdain, and possibly starvation, as historical examples show. That word is "poetry."

Thus Arnold Bennett, almost a century ago, in his little book *Literary Taste: How to Form It* (Bennett 69). No doubt he exaggerated just a bit. (I love the "historical examples.") But we take his point. I knew it, in fact, before I had found and read his words, knew it before I wrote what is (and shall remain) the longest essay of my life with the dread word squarely there in the title. But I had thought the problem was more recent, that, in the good old days, poetry was accorded its rightful place at the top of the literary tree. Well, we must push the good old days back a bit further,

I am afraid. Bennett's discussion of the matter leads me to suspect that poetry became "a name of fear" when the reading public expanded, mass magazines were founded, and the gap between high literature and popular texts began to widen — a century or more before Bennett wrote. The problem is still with us, though much has happened since Bennett's time.

He thought, himself, that the way to cure people of their poetry anxiety ("the fearful prejudice of the average lettered man against the mere form of verse") was to encourage them to read poems that had the virtues of fiction: to read Wordsworth's "The Brothers," which, he said, "is a short story, with a plain, clear plot. Read it as such" (74). Or, he suggested, "Elizabeth Browning's *Aurora Leigh*," which might be read as a very good novel but contained "nearly all the moods of poetry that exist: tragic, humorous, ironic, elegiac, lyric — everything" (79). In short, Bennett thought that poetry anxiety might be alleviated by beginning with poems that offered the pleasures of fiction, before moving into the more complex parts of the poetical canon. It is easy to make fun of Bennett. In this book, he actually laid out the cost of accumulating a basic library and a plan for the reader to acquire cultural capital at a total expense of twenty-eight pounds, zero shillings, and one penny. The Arnold Bennett that Virginia Woolf mocked and taught us to sneer at is very visible in this book. And yet, he was mainly right, I think, in the direction of his thinking. Poetry anxiety is real — as real as math anxiety — and as important. But the problem presents itself to us differently now, partly because we are situated in the wake of the most sustained and informed attempt ever made to solve the problem of teaching people how to read a poem: an attempt that took a very different direction from the one advocated by Bennett.

I believe that this attempted solution was not merely a failure but in fact made the situation worse. In the pages that follow I intend to demonstrate how some of the most learned and intelligent critics of the past century — from whom I learned much and to whom I owe a great deal — were seriously wrong about the subject they knew best. And I want to make a few suggestions about how to recover from the mess they made. Put more specifically, I believe that what we still call the *New* Criticism was bad for poets and poetry and really terrible for students and teachers of poetry. And I believe this even though I am convinced that most of the New Critics were smarter than I am, more learned in their subject, and capable of producing much more powerful arguments on behalf of their positions than I can produce against them. Against all this, I have only one claim — that it didn't work, that it turned out badly, despite the cogency of their arguments and the subtlety of their analyses. Because this is a long essay, I have broken it into several segments.

Poetry, Modernism, and the New Critics

Few people would deny that poetry now plays a very minor role in our culture. The New Critics did not want this to happen. They tried to make a case for the supreme importance of poetry, based on a supposed opposition between poetry and other ways of using language. Allen Tate, for instance, argued that "public speech has become heavily tainted with mass feeling. Mass language is the medium of 'communication,' and its users are less interested in bringing to formal order what is today called the 'affective state' than in arousing that state" (Stallman 55). This statement is not just typical but foundational for the New Criticism. Let us factor out of Tate's dense prose the crucial points:

- mass feeling is bad;

- mass feeling contaminates public speech, turning it into mass language;

- mass language arouses emotions;

- emotions should not be aroused but brought into "formal order."

The proper vehicle for bringing "formal order" out of emotion, according to Tate, is poetry. This position has much in common with T. E. Hulme's preference for what he called "classicism" over romanticism, with T. S. Eliot's notion of the "objective correlative," and with many other modernist theories of poetry. In Tate's writing — and this is obvious even in the brief quotation we are considering — there is a clear social position undergirding the aesthetic position. The masses are bad, dangerous, incapable of clear thought, and manipulated by the media of public communications. This is, in fact, a political position. The best word for it, though obsolete in American politics, is Tory. Tate's view is precisely that of the American Tories who sided with England in the American Revolution and maintained that those we still call patriots were merely demagogues. They were probably right to some extent, those Tories of old, but also wrong, and a more egalitarian United States emerged from that conflict. But my point is that Tate's views are indeed political and social, though wearing the mask of pure reason. Being political, of course, is not the same thing as being wrong, but it is wrong to claim that you are above politics when your views are actually political. It is also wrong to claim that you are an impartial judge when you despise those whose trial you are conducting, as was the case with the judge who presided over the trial of Sacco and Vanzetti in the twenties: "When the cases came to trial, Judge Webster Thayer said of Vanzetti 'this man, although he may not have actually committed the crime attributed to him, is nevertheless morally culpable, because he is the enemy of our existing institutions.' This was the same judge who would ask Professor James P. Richardson of Dartmouth College 'Did you see what I did to those anarchist bastards the other day? I guess that will hold them for a while'"(*The Guardian*, August 23, 1998). This may seem irrelevant to the question of poetry, but I assure you that it is indeed connected — and I promise to make that connection plain. But first, back to Tate and his view of poetry. His opposition between poetry as a private art and the language of mass communication will clash and clang throughout the following discussion.

In the time when Tate was writing, it seems to me, poetry played a much larger role in Anglo-American culture than it does today. Its diminished status is partly the result of displacement by the new media that Tate despised (though it may actually be embodied and alive in those media — in ways he would not acknowledge as poetical), but I would like to suggest that a lot of the damage has been done inside our schools and colleges, by well-intentioned teachers, so that we must look there to discover just what happened and to find some remedies. We need look for remedies, of course, only if we believe, as I do myself, that poetry can make important contributions to our lives as individuals and to the life of our language and our society. Poetry, in fact, does a lot of the same work as prose, but does it, in general, more powerfully and compactly, with more of what Tate called "formal order." It offers us textual pleasure in its formal qualities — a pleasure in the grace, vigor, or ingenuity of the language itself — but it also offers us expressive pleasure, in that it articulates our concerns and our situations. It speaks for us as well as to us. And finally, because of its memorability and brevity, it is a powerful medium of communication, a way of exchanging and sharing thoughts and feelings with others — sometimes, perhaps, even a means of persuasion.

In this essay I shall argue that we have lost the craft of reading poetry — lost sight of poetry's private pleasures and of its public powers — and that our methods of studying and teaching poetry for the past half-century are very much to blame for this condition. That is, English teachers, among whom I number myself — *we* English teachers, then — in our bumbling, well-meaning way, have done a lot of the damage, and we have done it both at the college level and at the level of secondary school. From this point on, then, I shall speak as an English teacher, addressing the problems of teaching poetry in the classroom and suggesting remedies at that level as well. But I want to begin this discussion with an example chosen from another source, an episode of failed instruction in the arts as represented in Marcel Proust's monumental novel, *In Search of Lost Time*. You will remember how it goes, in the first volume of Proust's work, when

M. Charles Swann tries to talk about poetry and painting to the woman with whom he is hopelessly in love.

> If, then, Swann tried to show her in what
> artistic beauty consisted, how one ought to
> appreciate poetry or painting, after a minute
> or two she would cease to listen, saying: "Yes
> . . . I never thought it would be like that." And
> he felt her disappointment was so great that
> he preferred to lie to her, assuring her that he
> had only touched the surface, that he had not
> time to go into it all properly, that there was
> more in it than that. Then she would interrupt
> with a brisk, "More in it? What? . . . Do tell
> me!", but he did not tell her, for he realized
> how petty it would appear to her, and how dif
> ferent from what she had expected, less sensa
> tional and less touching [*moins sensationnel et
> moins touchant*], he was afraid, too, lest, disillu
> sioned in the matter of art, she might at the
> same time be disillusioned in the greater mat
> ter of love. (Proust 185, ellipses in the origi
> nal)

We can, I believe, see the attitudes and concerns of many English teachers represented by those of Swann, however embarrassing that may be. He feels that his pupil is guilty of a number of errors of taste that he would like to correct. He is also, of course, terribly afraid of losing what he believes (quite mistakenly, of course) to be her love for him. English teachers are not, I hope, worried about their students remaining in love with them, but they are quite properly concerned about earning and keeping the respect of those students, without which they can accomplish little or nothing. But let us see what we can learn from the example of Swann. He tries, Proust tells us, "to show her in what artistic beauty consisted, how one ought to appreciate poetry." He is also trying, as the context makes clear, to correct her bad taste, to make her feel the right emotions for the right objects, but she is drawn to the touching and sensational, and hopes that her teacher will lead her to even more intense experiences of the same kind as those she already encounters in the heroic romances she likes to read. Put in terms of the problem we are considering, she is not a crafty reader but a naive one, reading only texts that make a direct, sensational appeal to her, or which she can read so as to experience that kind of pleasure. Her teacher suggests that other texts are better, greater than those she likes, and she is perfectly ready to entertain that suggestion, but she wants these "better" texts to give her the same sensations she has already learned to enjoy.

The problem for Swann, of course, is that his "better" texts are in fact less sensational, less sentimental, than those she enjoys. In the visual arts, for instance, he offers her the coolest and most restrained of painters, Vermeer of Delft, as an example. Her response? "She asked whether he had been made to suffer by a woman, if it was a woman that had inspired him, and once Swann told her that no one knew, she . . . lost all interest in that painter" (185). Certain contemporary novelists, as it turns out, are quite ready to gratify Odette's wishes, with books like *Girl with a Pearl Earring*, and there is even an opera, *Writing to Vermeer*, based on imaginary letters to the painter from his wife, his mother-in-law, and his model. As a reviewer in the *New York Times* pointed out, "it would take a mighty dose of imagination to turn Johannes Vermeer into the stuff of dramatic opera" (Riding 1). Odette, the backward pupil, was in fact seeking the postmodern, despite the resolute modernism of her "teacher." This is one of the things that should make her interesting to us. Wrong then and there, she might be right here and now. Let us at least consider the possibility, for she is the embodiment of our pedagogical problem — and our opportunity. We should notice that she commits all the fallacies that modernist critics and teachers have taught us to avoid — the affective, the intentional, the communicative, the biographical — while Swann, like those same teachers, tries to repress those powerful though "fallacious" responses by lecturing her on the nature of "artistic beauty." Swann, as it happens, is more like us than is usually perceived. He is writing an article about Vermeer (just as we might be writing an article about a writer we are teaching) which he hopes to publish one day, but which, like ours, alas, too often, may never, quite, get finished. And he wishes, as we may, to wean his student away from her vulgar, meretricious pleasures (think sitcoms, quiz shows, fanzines) and get her onto the solid food of serious art and literature. Welcome, we and Swann seem to be saying to our students, to high culture and its discontents!

M. Swann, I would like to suggest, is not only like us in general, he is like a specific sort of English teacher; or, to put it more tactfully, and perhaps more usefully, he should remind us of a certain specific approach to literary study, for Swann's approach to literature is very much like that of our own New Critics. There are good historical reasons for this. Proust himself was a major modernist, and the New Criticism arose in America directly from literary modernism, as embodied in the writings of Pound, Joyce, Eliot, and Ford Madox Ford — the "men of 1914," as they were called. Allen Tate was friendly with Ford, who has been described as his mentor (Vinh 33), and he was also, along with John Crowe Ransom, Cleanth Brooks, and Robert Penn Warren, a founder of the New Critical movement. The New Criticism, as the adjective *new* proclaims, was the academic and critical arm of British and American modernism, which owed a good deal to the Parisian modernism of Proust, Mallarmé, Valéry, de Gourmont, Laforgue, and others. Proust himself was undoubtedly in sympathy with Swann's perspective on art and literature. But my point is that Swann can stand for us as an exemplar of the New Criticism specifically because of the way that he condemns the literature that Odette likes as "sensational" and "touching." For these are pejorative terms in Swann's vocabulary and in that of the New Critics — and this fact is the source of many of the problems we face in trying to persuade our students that literary works are indeed sources of textual pleasure and power.

Odette, of course, is presented by Proust as liking only romantic fiction or texts that are touching and sensational in matters of romance. But Odette is herself a character *in* a love story called "Un Amour de Swann," or "Swann in Love," which is as touching and sensational as one could wish. If Swann were really a teacher instead of a rather pedantic lover, he should be offering her a craft of reading that connects stories like the one in which she is involved to the stories in which she likes to imagine herself. Of course, part of Odette's — and Swann's — difficulty here is that she sees their actual relationship in terms of her romantic reading. A more crafty reader would have a sharper sense of the difference between romances and actual life. That is one reason why the craft of reading is important. As I shall be arguing throughout this book, a major feature of that craft is the understanding of what kind of text one is reading. The New Critics, as we shall see, insisted on a distinction between good and bad poetry; whereas, in the craft of reading I am proposing, terms like *good* and *bad* make sense only with respect to works of the same kind — and there are many kinds of poetry. But our modernist, New Critical pedagogy was based on a quite different assumption, proposing an art of reading that required a certain sort of "art poem" and rejecting as inferior or unpoetical a whole range of texts, from poems of raw personal feeling to poems of collective political protest.

Here is the way Tate put it, describing the various kinds of bad poems being advocated and written around him: "political poetry for the sake of the cause; picturesque poetry for the sake of the home town; didactic poetry for the sake of the parish; even a generalized personal poetry for the sake of the reassurance and safety of numbers. This last I suppose is the most common variety, the anonymous lyricism in which the common personality exhibits its commonness, its obscure and standard eccentricity, in a language that seems always to be deteriorating" (Stallman 55). Even in his prose Tate is paradoxical. The common personality produces poetry that is at once standard and obscure, common and eccentric. Not content with condemning common poetry as trivial or banal, he must make it strange and difficult as well. Eccentric with respect to what center, we may wonder. He makes this claim, I think, because he wants to reserve for poetry all the power of expressing the truth, and he wants to believe that truth must be the possession of an elite, far removed from any situation in which "the common personality exhibits its commonness." The New Critics emphasized poetry and were most effective with poetry partly because it was there that they could make the case for a higher, purer art most successfuly. But it is their very success, I wish to argue, that lies at the root of our present problems in teaching a craft of reading that connects literature to life. That is why we must turn to poetry, and to the New Criticism, to solve those problems, and that is why I have chosen to begin this book with an essay on the craft of reading poetry.

As I indicated above, it is clear that poetry is being taught and studied less and less in our classrooms at present. And when it is taught, it is seldom taught effectively. This is partly due to a shift of interest and attention among English teachers at research universities. Structuralist and poststructuralist literary theory emphasized narrative and even philosophical texts, while treating poetry only in a highly formalistic and linguistic manner. Moreover, the recent move toward cultural studies has resulted in an emphasis on novels and the mass media, allowing poetry, for the most part, to remain in a belletristic corner. These shifts of interest have been justified, and I am not going to argue that this part of academic history could or should be undone. But teachers of cultural studies, in seldom attending to poetry, have made a crucial error. They have implicitly accepted the formalist and New Critical view of poetry. This critique of cultural studies is supported eloquently by Cary Nelson in *Repression and Recovery: Modern American Poetry and the Politics of Cultural Memory, 1910–1945* (1989), though his argument is made from a different angle from mine.

And it is worth pointing out that Stuart Hall, the dean of cultural studies, has warmly endorsed Nelson's position. Ignoring poetry is an error, in short, that can be rectified within cultural studies themselves, and has been addressed there. But Nelson's book is more than a decade old, and the situation of poetry in our classrooms has not improved. This is the case, I believe, because we have not yet done the job of historical analysis that must precede any real change in the craft of reading poetry. The development of such a craft will require going back and undoing certain attitudes toward the reading of poetry that are deeply rooted in our teaching practices. At the center of the problem, as it exists in American departments of English at all levels, are the doctrines of the New Critics. Which means that we will do well to reconsider the achievements of those critics and to examine more carefully the ways in which their good intentions contributed to the decline of interest in poetry, even as they were teaching a generation of scholars how to read more closely.

This charge will require some explanation. We all know that the New Critics privileged poetry and did some brilliant work in the exegesis of poetic texts, especially those by metaphysical poets, but also other kinds of poems that could be read in a metaphysical sort of way — and quite a few poems allow this kind of reading. Beyond that, however, their preference for subtlety and complexity, which went hand in hand with a sustained critique of the obvious and the sentimental, had the effect of cutting off the kind of poetry they liked from the more popular poems that had functioned to get many young people interested in poetry in the first place. And in a more insidious way, their preference for the subtle and complex had social and political ramifications. As we might expect, they criticized severely poems that were overtly political, and they ignored whole areas of popular song. They were open to the Scottish ballads from several centuries in the past but not to the blues being sung around them and adapted in poems by writers like Langston Hughes. This attitude may be attributed to nostalgia for the Old South in a group of men who had strong ties to that particular past, but that explanation, however valid it may be, seems less significant than one that points to the specifically modernist attitudes that their teaching expressed. We cannot explain the persuasiveness and durability of their ideas on regional grounds, for those ideas were adapted and have persisted across this entire country, through and beyond the civil rights movement. As things are now, we either do not teach poetry, or we teach it their way — which does not work for many students.

What I am calling modernist in their teaching — and I have been studying modernism for nearly half a century — can be reduced to a powerful opposition between the rhetorical and the poetical. This view was put succinctly by Yeats when he said that he made rhetoric from his quarrels with others and poetry from his quarrels with himself. "Rhetoric" in this modernist formulation signifies writing that is persuasive, interested, seeking to move the reader in a particular direction; whereas "poetry" signifies writing that is contemplative, disinterested, which hovers among possible directions, held immobile by irony, paradox, or ambiguity. Such a notion is rooted in Kant's *Critique of Judgment*, in which he defined art as "purposefulness without purpose" — a definition echoed in Arnoldian "disinterestedness" and strongly present in modernist formulations as well, sometimes expressed as a desire to write a book or poem about nothing. In contrast with this ideal of textual purity is the notion of rhetoric as vulgar, commercial, or political, always *interested* (in the bad sense of that word) and therefore never *interesting*. In the vocabulary of many modernists, including the New Critics, this often takes the form of an overt rejection of what is called "sentimental" or "sensational" and a more covert rejection of the public and political. The dignity of poetry requires those who teach it to accept the fact that, in Auden's famous formulation, it "makes nothing happen."

There are at least two things wrong with this view. One is that it is theoretically impossible. There is no zero degree of rhetoric in human language. One must go to mathematics for that. The other is that it is demonstrably untrue. The national epics of the Serbs, for example, still exert a powerful influence upon their thinking about Kosovo, and one could think about many other cases, closer to home. I know that poems and songs like "Strange Fruit," which I heard Josh White sing in a Greenwich Village nightclub when I was in college, helped to shape my own thoughts and feelings about racism, as they helped to drive the civil rights movement of later years. One can say that this kind of verse is not poetry, that it is rhetoric. That, I am afraid, would be the New Critical response. Which means that, if we are to connect poetry with life again and restore it to its proper place in our culture and our curriculum, we must reject the New Critical view. But I am getting ahead of my own argument here. For such rejection to be effective it must be informed, nuanced, and prepared to salvage as much as possible from the teachings of a group of critics who thought deeply and seriously about the nature of poetry and about the teaching of it.

The New Criticism had such a powerful and persistent influence mainly because it was presented in one of the most effective textbooks ever published in this country, Brooks and Warren's *Understanding Poetry*. That influence was extended by the neat fit between New Critical dogma and a certain approach to academic testing, but our investigation must begin with that powerful book itself. *Understanding Poetry* included the authors' appreciative analyses of a wide range of poems. It also included several analytical attempts to show why certain of them were "bad poems": such as Adelaide Anne Proctor's "The Pilgrims," Francis Mahony's "The Bells of Shandon," and Joyce Kilmer's "Trees." I think these attempts are not especially successful, but that is not the most important thing about them. What is important is that this attitude — the wholesale "correction" of popular taste — taken up and magnified in hundreds of classrooms across the country, had the effect of purging the curriculum of the very poems that had once functioned to give students textual pleasure, thus preparing them to take an interest in poetic texts that did not display their hearts so obviously on their verbal sleeves. Most children love simple songs, jingles, and nursery rhymes. The path from these to the poems we all admire goes through the kind of poetry the New Critics attacked so ferociously, so that their attacks had the result of cutting off the connection between the roots and the blossom, if I may borrow an image from a poem included in *Understanding Poetry*. Richard Eder, reviewing a book on Kipling in a recent *New York Times Book Review*, put it this way: "I memorized and recited 'Gunga Din' and

'Charge' at school. What a clangor they raise in the mouth and ear! Lacking such, perhaps, we can never be entirely tuned to the visual and intellectual clangors of more sophisticated and infinitely better poets" (Eder 16). I share these sentiments, but would demur at the notion that other poets are "infinitely better." Better in certain ways, perhaps, to the extent that sophisticated equals better, but not "infinitely better," no, not even close. How could an ordinary person, or even a crafty reader, begin to appreciate anything as good as all that?

This critical assault on the more popular and public sorts of literature was not only enshrined in that famous textbook by its justly famous authors. It was also carried on in the literary quarterlies and other periodicals, as well as in published books of critical essays. One of the most important and revealing of these critical assaults is the one we have already had occasion to notice, written by the poet-critic Allen Tate for the *Southern Review* in 1938, the same year the first edition of *Understanding Poetry* was published. After that it was reprinted in a number of important anthologies, including the New Critical Bible, R. W. Stallman's *Critiques and Essays in Criticism* (1949). In this essay, called "Tension in Poetry," Tate attacked (and I think *viciously* is not too extreme an adjective to describe his tone) a poem of Edna St. Vincent Millay's. In fact, the generalizations about poetry and mass language that we have already been considering lead directly into his critique of Millay's poem.

Before considering this critique, I want to clarify Tate's relationship to Brooks and Warren and to *Understanding Poetry*. Originally Tate and Warren were going to write a poetry textbook together, which Scribner's was interested in publishing. Tate asked Brooks to join

them, with a view to having Brooks replace him, because, as he said, "I fear otherwise the book will never
get done" (Vinh 28). Meanwhile, Brooks had ap-
proached Henry Holt and Company with a similar idea.
Ultimately, Tate dropped out — though Brooks tried
hard to keep him in (Vinh 29–30) — and Warren joined
Brooks for the Holt project, which became *Understanding
Poetry*. When "Tension in Poetry" appeared in the *Southern Review*, of which Brooks was an editor, he wrote Tate,
saying, "Your last piece for the Review was fine" (Vinh
46). We can legitimately read Tate's essay, then, as being
in sympathy with the view of poetry presented by
Brooks and Warren in their textbook, perhaps even de-
cisively influential on that view. In the essay Tate said
that the political message of the poem, with which he dis-
agreed, was not the motivation for his attack. Rather it
was the fact that the poem was a bad poem, a poem that
used language in the wrong way. He began his critique
by quoting the following lines from the poem:

> What from the splendid dead
> We have inherited —
> Furrows sweet to the grain, and the weed
>   subdued —
> See now the slug and the mildew plunder.
> Evil does overwhelm
> The larkspur and the corn;
> We have seen them go under.

Tate then proceeded in the following way:

> From this stanza by Miss Millay we infer that
> her splendid ancestors made the earth a good

place that has somehow gone bad — and you get the reason from the title: *Justice Denied in Massachusetts*. How Massachusetts could cause a general desiccation, why (as we are told in a footnote to the poem) the execution of Sacco and Vanzetti should have anything to do with the rotting of the crops, it is never made clear. These lines are mass language: they arouse an affective state in one set of terms, and suddenly an object quite unrelated to those terms gets the benefit of it; and this effect, which is usually achieved, as I think it is here, without conscious effort, is sentimentality. Miss Millay's poem was admired when it first appeared about ten years ago, and is no doubt still admired by persons to whom it communicates certain feelings about social justice, by persons for whom the lines are the occasion of feelings shared by them and the poet. But if you do not share those feelings, as I happen not to share them in the images of desiccated nature, the lines and even the entire poem are impenetrably obscure.

I am attacking here the fallacy of communication in poetry. (Stallman 56)

There is more, but I suppose this is enough. Tate attacked the "sentimentality" of "Miss" Millay's "mass language," charging it, as we might expect from his general views, with being both "impenetrably obscure" and guilty of the "fallacy of communication in poetry." Why the same devices used by many another elegiac poet should suddenly become obscure sentimental specimens of fallaciously communicative mass language may be a bit mysterious to present readers, especially if they are aware that Tate has taken these lines out of a context that justified them metaphorically. But my point is that the radical break between poetry and mass language postulated here by Tate ("the fallacy of communication"), and deployed so as to exclude even an accomplished poet like Millay, is a major clue to the way that the New Criticism operated to put poetry into an elite cultural ghetto, forever separated from ordinary human language and ordinary human concerns. I shall return to this aspect of the New Critical effect, and to Millay's poem, later on, but first I must discuss another aspect of that effect.

A second unfortunate result of the New Critical approach to poetry was the development of a set of technical terms that could be used as the basis for assignments. I'm thinking of *tone, irony, paradox, tension,* and the like — all useful words, to be sure — which came, in many classrooms, to be what poems and other literary works were all about. That is, instead of asking what a text had to do with us, its readers, we began asking about the role played by tone, irony, paradox, or symbolism in this or that poem. This is one place where we can make a clear distinction between reading as a craft and reading as an art. The New Critics tried to teach an art of reading poetry which required a definition of good poetry so narrow as to exclude poems that many people found expressive of their interests and concerns. Thus their art of reading privileged what we might call the "art poem" over the "life poem" — or rather, the art in the poem over the life in the poem. By following Brooks and Warren down the New Critical path of tone and tension, we English teachers succeeded in getting life itself, with all its embarrassing features, out of our classrooms and out of the poems we studied as well. We were comfortable with tone, irony, paradox, and symbolism, and the makers of standardized tests were even more comfortable with them. Poetry, in the hands of the standardized testers, could serve as a vehicle to determine which students could find symbols, detect the presence of paradoxes, and perform other functions amenable to testing by multiple-choice questions and grading by machines. This formidable machinery continues to rumble along even today. And poetry, which, as Robert Frost said, is what gets lost in translation, gets even more lost on our educational assembly lines. But let me illustrate this more concretely.

Misunderstanding Poetry

The Internet giant America Online offers bulletin boards on which students can post questions and ask for assistance. I spent some time a while ago, lurking on their high school English bulletin boards, and even offering advice occasionally. I would like to share with you some of the postings I have seen, unedited, and then analyze them as symptoms of our pedagogical problems. I have grouped them under the headings of symbols, tone, irony, and theme.

Symbols

> Subject: rose for emily
> I need help identifying the symbolism in this story! Thanks!

Subject: huck finn-symbolism of river

I am writing a paper on the symbolism of the Mississippi River in Huck Finn. How is the river a symbolic mother to Huck? I need examples from the book too. Please help fast.

Subject: symbolism: gardens

what do gardens symbolize? are there any sexual inuendos? anything that one could dig up on the symbolism of gardens would be of great help. thanks

Let me make a few comments on these before moving on to tone. I especially like the idea that one might *dig up* some symbolism of gardens. I also like the idea of "sexual innuendos" lurking in gardens. With all those bees and flowers around, there ought to be *something* sexy about gardens. I'm quoting these calls for help, however, not to make fun of the students who wrote them but for what they reveal about the courses (and the teachers) that inspired them. It is plain that a lot of questions are being asked about symbols and symbolism in these students' classes. Faulkner's "A Rose for Emily," after all, is about sex — no garden symbolism needed — and about pride, about human longing. Instead of talking about those things, however, students are being encouraged to talk about "symbolism." This kind of talk is one of the things that turns students off: one of the things that proclaims the separation of school-talk from any kind of life-talk. The question about *Huck Finn* is perhaps even worse, since the student has already been told that the river is a "symbolic mother" to Huck and is now desperately trying to find out "how" — please help fast, that student says, 'cause Ol' Man River just keeps on rollin' along. My point is simply that if we are going to keep on teaching these works, we have got to find ways of discussing them and assigning papers about them that are less artificial, closer to the lives of our students and ourselves, and just less phony. But let us move on now, to tone.

Tone

Subject: "Antigone"
How do I decide the Tone of Antigone?

How indeed? How could a complex drama like that have a single tone? And who would really care? *Antigone* is about important matters: pride, respect, honor, and a clash between religious values and political values. It can be connected in all sorts of ways to issues and feelings that are alive and important in our world. To ask about its "tone" is to take the play out of the real world and put it squarely in the artificial world of "English class," where nothing real is allowed to enter. This world, dominated by academic clichés and driven by the convenience of testers, simply turns the poor students off and drives many of the others to find the answers in notes, whether online or in books, instead of reading the work and trying to discover what it may have to say to them as human beings. Now irony.

Irony

Subject: Oedipus Rex — Irony
I need help finding Irony in Oedipus

Rex! There's supposedly a lot in there, but I've been assigned Scene II and there's only so much . . .

What a terrible thing it is to be required to find irony in *Oedipus Rex*, knowing that there's "a lot in there," and then be given a scene that got short-changed on this precious stuff. It is, one might almost say, ironic. Now this is a play about how a scandal in a ruler's private life is causing public disasters — like a plague, for instance. You might think that questions about the relation between sex and politics, between private and public life, would have a certain resonance in these times. Questions about justice, guilt, responsibility, sexual desire, and family life are raised by the play. But "irony" is a safe topic, a "literary" topic, one of those topics that seems to belong only to the artificial world of "English classes," where we English teachers feel at home. My point is that, by playing it "safe," we are losing the game. The great works of literature are worthy of our attention only if they speak to our concerns as human beings, and these must take precedence over the artificial concerns of symbol, tone, and irony. Symbol, tone, and irony, after all, are only devices, or ways of talking about technique. We need, and shall have to find, better ways of talking about what these works mean and how they connect to our lives. Which brings me to the question of theme.

Theme

Subject: HUCK FINN
    Can someone please tell what chapter 42 is about? What is the theme?

> Subject: Analytical reading class
> I have to write a book review and we
> have to differenciate between plot and theme.
> Help! What is a theme exactly?

These students are crying for help: "What is the theme?" says one, and, "What is a theme exactly?" says another. Now I doubt very much that their teachers never told them what a theme was, but for some reason they didn't get it or can't apply what they got to actual works, or don't find the question interesting enough to make the effort. The word *theme* itself seems to interfere with the reading process. Like those other words — *symbol, tone, irony* — the word *theme* turns a subtle process into a thing that can be quantified ("there's . . . a lot in there") or dug up. In our classrooms, these words have been woven into a screen, a special kind of texture or text that stands between the literature students read and their own humanity. In directing them to look for "theme" we have made it difficult for them to find life in the works they read. The "art of reading" developed by the New Critics has become formulaic in our classrooms. We have managed to make reading seem too difficult and to trivialize it at the same time. Here is one more glimpse into a contemporary classroom:

> Subject: Ox-bow Incident
> What are the historical references of
> The Ox-bow Incident other than the Holo-
> caust in general? Any specifics? Are there
> any sites that analyze the book? My teacher
> likes to discuss, and I'm having a hard time
> enjoying the book, so reading between the
> lines is a little tough for me. Thanks!

This teacher likes to discuss, which sounds like a good thing in general, but this student is feeling some pressure to prepare for that discussion in a certain way, which is referred to in this plea as "reading between the lines." In this case a novel about a lynching in the Old West has to be read, between the lines, as a historical reference to the "Holocaust in general." First of all, just how a book published in 1940 might be supposed to refer to the Holocaust in general is, shall we say, open to question. And it is not as if we are lacking examples of lynching or vigilante justice closer to home than the genocidal practices of Nazi Germany. One might connect this narrative to a poem/song like "Strange Fruit," for example. *The Ox-Bow Incident* is a novel rather than a poem, which may explain why the teacher is trying to historicize the text, but to do that one must know a little history, including the history of the text under consideration. But I don't want to quibble about exactly what is to be found "between the lines" in this novel. My point is rather that "between the lines" is another one of those notions woven into the text we have placed between our students and the works of literature they are reading.

Now I want to suggest that my little excursion into the netherworld of online help reveals, more than anything else, the powerful influence still exercised on the study and teaching of poetry by that sixty-three-year-old textbook *Understanding Poetry*. The terminology of irony, symbol, and theme is the terminology of Brooks and Warren. This critical vocabulary, as I see it, has operated to cut poems off from their subject matter and their possible connection with the lives of their readers, just as the assault on "the fallacy of communication" worked to open up a gap between the intelligible and the "sophisticated." It is this gap that must be bridged if poetry is to resume its proper place in our culture and our schools. And I am suggesting that it is helpful to think of it as a gap between an art of reading that has turned into a technology and a craft of reading that should resist this process because it expects readers to read as different individuals and admits that poems, like other texts, may both please and persuade — that they may be for use and not merely for contemplation.

With this in mind, let us go back to *Understanding Poetry*. In many ways, Brooks and Warren were acutely aware of this situation themselves, and tried to address it in their introduction to the book. There they suggested (in the first edition, 1938) that poetry satisfies the same "human interests and impulses" as those which people normally satisfy in the following ways: "They listen to speeches, go to church, listen to radio programs, read magazine stories, or the gossip columns of newspapers" (25). Poetry, say Brooks and Warren, is concerned with "the same impulses and interests," but "good poetry, and good literature in general, give a fuller satisfaction to those impulses and interests" (25). Here, stated very clearly, is their version of what I have called the Swann/ Odette problem. As they present the problem, the human needs to be satisfied (impulses and interests) are the same, but are satisfied more fully by "good" poetry and "good" literature than in popular textual forms. They may be right, but this is far from being a simple matter. It is certainly an important one, however, which requires further investigation. The same statement persists in later editions of *Understanding Poetry*, with such minor changes as the substitution of television for radio. Let us think about it for a moment.

Does good poetry offer more of the same kind of satisfaction as gossip columns and sitcoms? Or does it satisfy some other needs? As the Swann/Odette example suggests, some people believe that there are important differences between the satisfactions of sensational texts and those of aesthetic texts. Allen Tate is clearly one of those people, and Swann is another. It is shocking to move from Tate's attack on "mass language" to the insistence of his close friends Brooks and Warren on a continuum from gossip columns to good poetry — unless all of the New Critical disdain for sentimentality and "the fallacy of communication" is hidden in that word *good*, thus masking a difference in kind by an apparent difference in degree. It seems clear, in any case, that Millay's poem would not count as "good" under this aesthetic regime.

Many of us today would argue — as I believe we should argue — that there is a definite continuum between ordinary language, mass language, and poetic language. I regard any attempt to seal off the purely poetic from the sentimental and the communicative as a theoretical error that leads to serious pedagogical problems. We might think of it as "the fallacy of noncommunication." If poetry does not communicate, it becomes the Mandarin discourse of a comfortable elite. As we have seen, Brooks and Warren were aware of this problem, but they could not avoid the critical disdain articulated by Allen Tate. Thus their powerful textbook nodded toward mass culture and its powers in the introduction but moved away from it throughout the book. I have already mentioned the way the use of the term *good* in relation to poetry and literature led Brooks and Warren to critical attacks on popular poems in *Understanding Poetry* and to a general attitude of disparagement toward ordinary and popular uses of poetry similar to that expressed so vigorously by Tate. By "ordinary and popular" I mean to indicate a range of uses from the highly personal to the public and collective. The extent of this range is in fact a measure of just how much the New Critics excluded from the domain of "good" poetry. But let me be more specific.

By personal poetry I mean such things as the way that Vera Brittain, her fiancé, and her brother expressed themselves naturally in poetry during World War I, sending their thoughts and feelings to one another in poems as well as letters until both of the men died in the war. I doubt whether Brooks and Warren would find many of their poems "good," and I know that Tate would have found them sentimental, but they obviously afforded the writers a certain kind of textual pleasure, and they are still interesting to a sympathetic reader. They constitute one of the kinds of writing that connect the more obvious sorts of popular text to the "good" poetry admired by Brooks and Warren. By public and collective, I mean such things as Millay's poem about Sacco and Vanzetti, which first appeared in a collection of poems by various writers protesting the executions of those two men. I will discuss the poem and its context more fully later on. For the moment it is enough to note that by taking Millay's poem out of its textual context — and its historical context — Tate has tried to make it seem isolated and unintelligible. He argues that you must share her politics to appreciate Millay's poem, but I would say that you can appreciate the controlled emotional power of the poem for its own sake, even if you believe that Sacco and Vanzetti had a fair trial — which, by the way, even those who think at least one of them guilty find it hard to claim.

But my main point about public and collective poetry is that it has an honorable position in the history of American poetry. Cary Nelson has expressed this position eloquently in a discussion of Millay's poem about the Nazi extermination of the Czechoslovakian village of Lidice, *The Murder of Lidice,* which was written for the radio and broadcast by NBC. Here is his conclusion:

> *The Murder of Lidice* raises interesting issues about the special public functions of poetry in periods of historical crisis. It is also linked with all the political poetry addressed to a mass audience in America — from the abolitionist poetry of the mid-nineteenth century through the poetry of Whitman, Lindsay, Sandburg, and Hughes. It is not the noble task of literary history to tell us we need not trouble ourselves to read *The Murder of Lidice.* If we wish to achieve some mixture of distance and identification in our relation to the politically persuasive poetry of our own moment, if we wish to know what poetry might have meant to its varied audiences in the past and to remain open to its different cultural functions in the present, we need to know the history of the genre in our own culture. (Nelson 42–43)

I could not agree more. The craft of reading poetry begins with the recognition that poems can serve different purposes and come in many genres. The New Criticism, by equating "good" poetry with a restricted set of generic possibilities, cut it off, not only from political or engaged poems, but from other forms of popular poetry as well. As Nelson puts it, "When we include Langston Hughes's (1902–1967) spiritual-, blues-, and jazz-influenced poetry in the canon, it becomes intellectually indefensible to exclude (as nonliterary) verses by, say, Gertrude "Ma" Rainey (1886–1939) or Bessie Smith (1896–1937)" (Nelson 66).

Brooks and Warren knew that poetry was connected to ordinary life, but they were uncertain what to do with this knowledge. Still, their concern is obvious in their conclusion to the introduction to the first edition of *Understanding Poetry*:

> But the fundamental point, namely, that poetry has a basis in common human interests, must not be forgotten at the beginning of any attempt to study poetry.
>
> The question of the value of poetry, then, is to be answered by saying that it springs from a basic human impulse and fulfils a basic human interest. To answer the question finally, and not immediately, one would have to answer the question as to the value of those common impulses and interests. But that is a question which lies outside of the present concern. As we enter into a study of poetry it is only necessary to see that poetry is not an isolated and eccentric thing, but springs from the most fundamental interests which human beings have. (1938, 25)

How different the word *common* sounds in their prose compared with Tate's. But their views are perhaps not so far from his as they may seem. By the third edition (1960), they had added something to the first sentence that is worth our notice:

> But the fundamental points, namely, that poetry has a basis in common human interests, *that the poet is a man speaking to men, and that every poem is, at center, a little drama,* must not be forgotten at the beginning of any attempt to study poetry. (addition in italics, 1960, 22)

The sexist language ("man speaking to men") introduced in this revision may seem like a minor matter, but it is not. There is a persistent strain of misogyny running through the thinking of "the men of 1914" and their followers. It is apparent in the way Tate treated Millay's poem, rather than attacking, for example, a similar poem by John Dos Passos; it is detectable in the selection and treatment of poems in *Understanding Poetry;* and, perhaps more significant, it is a part of the very theory of poetic value developed by the New Critical modernists. The quality — "sentimentality" — that Tate assigned to "Justice Denied in Massachusetts" was thought of by him (and by Brooks and Warren, as we shall see) as a specifically female mode of thought — or, rather, of feeling usurping the place of thought. That is why it is important for him to refer to the poet as "Miss" Millay. And that is why it became difficult for the New Critics to deal with the emotions adequately in their criticism. The most sensitive critic among them — and I have no doubt that it was Cleanth Brooks — must have felt this. We shall return to this concern in a moment, but first we should pause and look more closely at the way women poets were treated in the first edition of *Understanding Poetry*.

By my count there were ninety-four named poets anthologized in that textbook. Of these five were women. Moreover, one of those five, Adelaide Anne Proctor, was represented by a single poem that was included only to receive a devastating critique that begins with the oracular pronouncement that, although Charles Dickens admired her, "most modern readers of poetry would find this poem bad," and continues to claim that only readers guilty of "an uncritical and sentimental piety" could like the poem, whereas a "truly pious person who was also an experienced reader of poetry" would find the poem "stupid, trivial, and not worthy of the subject" (334). These guys did not mince words. In fairness I should add that Amy Lowell's one poem, "Patterns," receives a long, appreciative analysis that draws attention to its "unity," "thematic development," and the way that objects mentioned in the poem become "symbols" (142). One of the two poems by Emily Dickinson in the anthology also receives an appreciative reading. Two short imagist poems by H.D. are discussed along with two lines by Ezra Pound, though Pound's two lines receive most of the editors' attention. And the two by Elizabeth Barrett Browning escape unscathed. Altogether, however, there are only eight poems by women out of a list of nearly three hundred, which I make out to be a bit more than 2 percent of the total. And poets who spoke for racial or ethnic minorities, like Countee Cullen and Langston Hughes, just don't appear at all. It is no doubt reasonable to speak of racism and sexism in connection with this selection of poems, but for our purposes, it is even more important to note that this selection works to eliminate voices emerging from popular culture and voices articulating political thoughts and feelings of all sorts.

To return, now, to the passage added to the conclusion of the introduction to *Understanding Poetry*, I read this interpolated passage as evidence that Brooks and Warren were becoming aware that this book could lead teachers — was leading teachers — to an excessive emphasis on the formal aspects of poetry. I would argue further that they must have seen this as a possible response from the beginning, for this whole concluding section to their introduction, even in the first edition, betrays this concern in its clumsy reiteration of crucial phrases (in the first passage above, "basic human impulse . . . basic human interest . . . common impulses and interests . . . fundamental interests"). I read the manner of this statement, along with the matter, as signs that the authors were troubled by what they were doing or uncomfortable in the doing of it. That is, either they sensed that their analytical methodology might supplant the human concerns that are the ultimate value of poetry, or they were embarrassed by their own approach to the sentimental in this paragraph. What they perhaps could not sense (or did not care about) was that, by their disparagement of the sentimental, as opposed to the ironic or paradoxical, they had made the typical modernist move of assigning feeling to the female and thought to the male, and by their rejection of the rhetoric of protest, they had ruled out the possibility of hearing the voices of those who felt ignored or oppressed by the dominant culture. Nor could they foresee the way that, in an age of technology and commodification, their methods would be debased and packaged at the expense of those human interests of which they spoke in such clumsy prose.

That this happened is one reason why I think we need to go back to the New Critics to salvage what was lost, even as we seek to restore some of their insights and methods to our curricula. But we also need to follow the clues in that final statement and consider how we may rediscover the role of "fundamental human interests" in our teaching of poetry, because poetic pleasure, as Brooks and Warren well knew, has to do with the ways these interests are given textual form. If we look at the table of contents of any edition of *Understanding Poetry*, we can see that the editors selected a great many poems that were quite accessible and offered recognizable human situations and impulses for consideration. But there are serious problems in the categories of poetry selected and the way the poems were organized and framed with questions and discussions. In the first edition the poems were grouped under the following headings: Narrative Poems, Implied Narrative, Objective Description, Metrics, Tone and Attitude, Imagery, and Theme. (In later editions these categories were modified — but only slightly — and two new sections were added, one simply called Poems for Study, and the other a fascinating section on How Poems Come About: Intention and Meaning.) If one is studying poetry as a formal discipline, this arrangement makes some sense, but in practice it had the result of making things like tone, imagery, and theme the major focus of a literary pedagogy in which those important human interests and impulses regularly got lost. Moreover, the list of categories reveals that certain kinds of poetry simply had no place in this collection. We get narration and description, but we do not get persuasion and argument. And even in description we get "Objective" but not "Subjective." (In the third edition the "Objective" is dropped.) Subjectivity creeps in as "Tone and Attitude," but this list tries awfully hard to sustain T. S. Eliot's notion that poetry must provide an "objective correlative" for any subjective emotion. And it is clearly based on the Yeats/Auden view that poetry makes nothing happen and shouldn't even try. (How good for us it is that their poems often paid little or no attention to their doctrine.)

Given this pedagogical history and the fact that these dogmas are still widely accepted, how, in fact, can we reconnect the study of poetry to the human interests and impulses that even Brooks and Warren understood were vital to it? We can do so, I should think, not by declaring an impassable gap between the texts of sensation and sentiment and the "good" poems that are properly to be admired, but by showing how all these works are part of the same order of poetic textuality—an order that requires a broadly based craft of reading to be understood. It is too easy, of course, to pontificate abstractly about these matters, so I shall end this essay by trying to demonstrate what I think we must do to restore poetry to a more central place in the teaching of English in colleges and schools. Put simply, we must select from a fuller range of poetic texts, and we should present them in a way that encourages readers to connect the poems to their lives. Most poems of real interest are about the scenes of life, scenes of language, that we encounter and inhabit in our daily lives, or about the great issues that move us to collective action. We are like Samuel Beckett's character Watt, who "desired words to be applied to his situation, . . . to the house, to the grounds, to his duties, to the stairs, to his bedroom, to the kitchen, and in a general way to the conditions of being in which he found himself" (Beckett 81). We want, we appreciate, we take pleasure in the application of words to our situations — and that includes our public concerns and commitments as well as our private joys and sorrows. We need a curriculum in poetry that responds to these needs.

Toward a Craft of Reading Poetry

Undoubtedly, the best way to establish such a curriculum is the way of Brooks and Warren. We need a new textbook that embodies a new craft of reading poems and offers a fuller range of poems to read. Nothing like that can be proposed or enacted within the confines of the present essay, but I cannot conclude having offered only critiques and generalizations. I must try, however briefly and inadequately, to give a few examples of the craft of reading I am proposing, after which I will sum up a few of the rules of thumb that every crafty reader of poetry should keep in mind. In any introductory course or textbook on the craft of reading poetry, there should be one or more sections devoted to a range of poems by a single poet. And, when I say "range," I mean just that — not just a half-dozen poems creamed off a life-work of hundreds, but a range that shows the different kinds of situations to which the poet applied his or her craft, from the humble and personal to the great and monumental — if the poet's range extends so far. From the private to the public, if the poet worked in both modes. But it will be better to illustrate than go on generalizing.

I would favor beginning by devoting a lot of time to a single poet whose poems clearly emerge from and connect to the ordinary events of human life. I think of Robert Herrick, for example, who regularly wrote about whatever was on his mind, whether a public event like King Charles I and his army's pursuing Essex into Cornwall in 1644, for which Herrick wrote a poem of welcome, or matters more private, trivial, and intimate. (I have suggested Herrick before, in a book called *The Rise and Fall of English*, and must apologize to any reader sufficiently acquainted that work to have a sense of *déjà lu* in considering the rest of this paragraph.) When his physician told him to stop drinking his favorite wine, Herrick wrote a mournful dirge, "His Fare-well to Sack," which begins, "Farewell thou Thing, time past so knowne, so deare / To me as blood to life and spirit . . ." and so on, with excessive and lugubrious lamenting for more than fifty witty lines. And when he was taken off this strict regime and allowed to drink sack again, he composed "The Welcome to Sack," a mock-epic poem of nearly a hundred lines, in which he compares himself to Ulysses (among other gods and heroes) returning home never to stray again. To follow a single poet like Herrick, or Robert Frost, or Marianne Moore, or Edna Millay, to get to know something about the poet's life as well as about the way the poet writes and the things he or she writes about, is one sure way to break down the barrier between literature and life. In the case of Herrick, we will find him complaining about the "warty incivility" of a river in Devon and the "churlish" neighbors he had when he lived there; we will also find him, at his best perhaps, thinking about the clothing and bodies of women he loves — or imagines he loves; we will find him in prayer; and finally we will observe him getting ready to die. And always we will find him turning to verse as his best and nearest means of expression.

One of my personal favorites is a nasty attack on a fellow named Skoles in four lines:

Upon Skoles

Skoles stinks so deadly, that his Breeches
    loath
His dampish Buttocks furthermore to cloath:
Cloy'd they are up with Arse; but hope, one
    blast
Will whirle about, and blow them thence at
    last. (2: 207)

For some reason this poem did not make it into the first edition of *Understanding Poetry*, though nine other poems by Herrick did, shrinking to three in the third edition. But even in the first edition, the two questions for students after "The Bad Season Makes the Poet Sad" invited them to write about "tone and attitude" and the symbolism of the last line. (The symbolism of the last line of "Upon Skoles" would be another matter.) And this is the point. The poems of Herrick, carefully selected, can be used to illustrate all the formal themes of *Understanding Poetry*, but a fuller range of them will reveal a writer with a nasty streak (and, yes, Skoles is how I say my name — I'm tempted to take the poem personally) who pays attention to bodily functions in a way that is almost frighteningly different from our own culture's sanitized treatment of the body. Herrick wrote an epigram about a laundress (named Sudds) who washed the clothes in piss and starched them in phlegm. And here is one about a woman named Joan or Jone, counting the sparse hairs on her head:

On Jone

Jone wo'd go tel her haires; and well she
  might,
Having but seven in all; three black, foure
  white. (2: 155)

Not nice, Herrick. But we need to consider his nasty epigrams along with his more famous poems about Julia in silks and Corinna celebrating Mayday if we are to get a sense of what his craft was — how he *used* poetry. If I were teaching the craft of reading poetry based on Herrick's work, I would certainly encourage students to produce their own epigrams, however outrageous, provided that they follow Herrick's rhyme and rhythm closely. It is when we compose in a strict form like this that we need to understand English metrics, and it is only after we understand this craft as writers that we can appreciate, as readers, just how skilled Herrick was at keeping a strict meter running while varying it with the rhythms of actual speech. His phrase "three black, foure white" has an economy that mimics the sparseness of the "haires" themselves. It falls within the range of the ta-dum, ta-dum meter but makes the "ta" and the "dum" almost equal. (Ideally, technical terminology like "iambic pentameter couplet" should come after the concept, when one sees the need for naming this kind of rhyme and rhythm.) The craft of reading poetry includes the form of verse. But we should not forget that this epigram, like the one on Skoles, is an insult, a rather brutal put-down of a victim. This one depends for its effect on exaggerating the fewness of the hairs. We might think of it as seventeenth-century trash-talking. Learning how to treat such texts, and how to compose modern equivalents, is part of the larger craft of reading poetry.

Starting with simple, even brutal, little poems is one way to get over the notion that poetry is some delicate precious thing that always requires "reading between the lines." One rule of thumb should be to begin reading not looking for something between or behind the lines but focusing on the lines themselves, always looking for prose sense, paying attention to punctuation, just as one does in reading anything else. Getting beyond the obvious sense means wondering whether the thinness of Jone's hair isn't being exaggerated here. Exaggeration is one of the simplest forms of irony. It affords us a pleasure in the way the language exceeds what we assume to be the realities of the situation. And, of course, it annoys the victims (poor Skoles, poor Jone) because it works like visual caricature, by exaggerating a feature that is an observable weakness or defect. Herrick may be inventing these people and their defects for the sheer pleasure of the exaggeration — but I would rather think that they are real. We need not know the answer, of course, and that answer may be beyond the reach of biographical scholarship in any case. Still, read enough poems by Herrick and you begin to wonder what he was like, how he lived, what his times were like. Modern readers may be startled that a clergyman, which he was, would write so many poems like his ten lines "Upon the Nipples of *Julia's* Breast" or his tributes to drink, but he wrote most of those poems (collected as *Hesperides*) when he did not hold a clerical post, writing more of his religious verse *(Noble Numbers)* later on. Still, he was never a Puritan, and in fact was booted out of his church in 1647, after Cromwell's victory in the civil war. In writing (a poem, of course) about his banishment from his post, he chose to regard his years in the vicarage as an exile from the city he loved, and the loss of his vicarage in Devon and his return to London not as an exile but as a return to "thee, blest place of my Nativitie," thus reversing his actual situation in the celebratory poem "His Returne to London" (2: 233). When Charles II was restored to the throne in 1660, however, Herrick went back to Devon, as one of his biographers says, "gratefully and graciously" (1: cviii), and remained quietly there until his death in 1674.

In lingering thus over Herrick's life and work I mean to suggest that the craft of reading poetry may be fostered by just such a process — staying with a single poet, learning about his or her life and times, emulating this poet's forms and topics. This will work best with a poet who has some range, and whose poems can attract the reader without long apologies or explications from a teacher. I have proposed Herrick because I am fond of his work and feel affectionate toward this individual who combined the jolly and the nasty, the erotic and the pious, so elaborately in his life and work — and who gave fifteen minutes of infamy to my cousin Skoles. But there are aspects of poetry one doesn't get with Herrick, which means that other poets and their work might well be used to replace or supplement his. If I were making a textbook on the craft of reading poetry, I would certainly try starting with an extensive selection from Herrick, framed with the right sort of questions and projects. One would find out soon enough whether it worked. In any case, however, many other poems and poets would be needed to get at the craft of reading poems.

I can easily imagine doing something similar with Langston Hughes, whose poetry circles continually around his situation as a writer of mixed race and ethnicity in a racist America, during a time in which Harlem became a center for cultural, artistic, and political activity. His much anthologized "Theme for English B" shows how, for a young man of his background, the personal was inevitably political and the private always, to some extent, public. Furthermore, because he worked so often in forms close to or borrowed from popular music, especially blues and jazz, the poetry of Hughes opens the door to the consideration of how the words and music of these popular forms function as poetry. I imagine a scene (perhaps from my own life, perhaps invented) in which an old professor totters into a poetry classroom with a stack of records and reverently plays a series of ballads collected in Scotland or Appalachia as a prelude to reading "Sir Patrick Spens" or "The Twa Corbies." And I superimpose upon that scene another in which more recent forms of words set to music are used in a similar way. In the case of Hughes we are fortunate enough to have available recordings of the music he heard sung by some of the people he heard sing it. I say Hughes "opens the door" because I see the possibility of all sorts of contemporary verbal performances that emphasize rhyme and rhythm following him into the room for study. Performance is just one aspect of poetry, but verse written to be sung, or rhythmic speech composed in the process of performance, is a part of the contemporary poetical scene — and part of the heritage of poetry in this language as well. We must attend to this if we are going to develop a craft of reading poetry for the present time. And by "attend to it," I mean that we must consider what particular texts are saying, whom they are addressing, and whom they are claiming to speak for or represent. We must be receptive but also mindful and critical, asking how any particular text connects to life as it is lived, and discussing the rights and wrongs of whatever views it represents.

I am in some danger here of trying to develop a whole craft of reading poetry in an essay intended to accomplish no more than point in the direction of such a craft. As I indicated earlier, it would take a textbook comparable to *Understanding Poetry* to provide a practical demonstration of such a craft. I will conclude, then, by simply sketching out the main outlines of such a craft and then providing some examples of how this craft might be practiced. Here, then, are the main aspects of the craft of reading poetry:

- Reading poetry is a branch of reading in general. A poem should be read first for its prose sense, with attention to all punctuation marks, including spacing and layout. Every word should be understood. Unfamiliar words or words that seem to be used strangely should be given special attention. So should groups of words that form a pattern, coming from the same source or pointing in the same direction.

- Reading begins with situating the text: asking what kind of poem this is, where it comes from, who is speaking, who is being addressed, what the situation is in which these words are uttered or about which they have been spoken.

- If the situation or context is unfamiliar, find out about it. Discuss it with other people. Look it up. The poet's life and world are relevant.

- To the extent that the poem is aimed at persuading the reader, consider whether you are persuaded or not, and then consider your reasons.

- To the extent that the poem seems aimed at generating an emotion, identify it and consider the extent to which you share that emotion and your reasons for accepting or resisting that invitation.

- To the extent that the poem addresses a condition of being or represents a human event, consider whether it speaks for you, applies to your condition, or not.

- Poems want to be valued — or poets want this for them. Ask yourself and others how they feel about this poem. Do you — or they — like it, admire it, despise it, remain indifferent to it? Discuss the reasons for these responses.

- Finally, consider what the form of the poem — the specific words, the figures of speech, the use of rhyme or rhythm, the relation of the sounds to the sense of the poem — has to do with the way you have received and evaluated the poem's thoughts and feelings.

These are simply the basic procedures of the craft, like the maxim of carpenters — "measure twice, cut once" — that every apprentice learns. It's a good rule, it will save you from cutting twice, but it will not make you a good craftsman. That comes from practice and practice alone. So I will conclude this discussion by practicing the craft a little bit, just to illustrate the points outlined above. You will have noticed that I avoided mentioning most of the favorite New Critical topics and devices, such as symbol, tone, and irony. This was not because poems have nothing to do with these things but because these things have come to loom too large in our discussions of poetry. Most writing — and most speech — requires attention to tone and attitude. Irony is not a mechanical trick but a quality that modulates or complicates the directness of statements. In listening to a speaking voice we always pay attention to the tone in which the words are spoken, because the emotion is often more present in the tone of voice than in the words. To speak of tone in a written text is to use a metaphor to describe something that is not literally there. Tone, in writing, consists of verbal cues for the vocal tone to be used in saying the words aloud. Good writing, whether in verse or in prose, provides these cues for the reader. For the New Critics, writing that uses such cues too blatantly or simplistically must be bad. We may wish to go along with them about this to some extent, but I would urge caution in employing such totalizing terms. We are not really dealing with good or bad in any absolute sense here, but with better or worse for certain specific occasions, audiences, and purposes.

With respect to tone and irony, I believe that careful attention to meaning will lead us to them in a more nuanced way than the direct approach (find the irony in

Oedipus) which we noticed in the students' cries for help above, and which I attribute to the standardization of a New Critical methodology. When it comes to symbols, we are in the area that one student called "reading between the lines," in which the students look for what they call the "secret-hidden-deeper-meaning" or "what the teacher knows and you don't." The approach by way of symbols has the practical effect of turning poems into cryptograms that always mean something different from what they seem to mean "on the surface." Using this approach it is all too easy to leap to some supposed second level of meaning (*The Ox-Bow Incident* is about the Holocaust) and lose sight of — or never arrive at — the primary level. In poems that have such a second level — and not all poems do — it usually depends on a clear understanding of the primary level, so that actually a third level is generated by the combination or interaction of the first two. This had better be illustrated quickly, since it threatens to outcomplicate the complications of the New Criticism itself. Let's look at a poem.

Pitcher

His art is eccentricity, his aim
How not to hit the mark he seems to aim at,

His passion how to avoid the obvious,
His technique how to vary the avoidance.

The others throw to be comprehended. He
Throws to be a moment misunderstood.

Yet not too much. Not errant, arrant, wild,
But every seeming aberration willed.

Not to, yet still, still to communicate
Making the batter understand too late.
(Robert Francis, in Wallace 172)

How should a crafty reader read this poem? Situate, situate. The "pitcher" in question is not a jug but a person who "throws" to a "batter." We are in the world of baseball here, which, if you are a North American of the early twenty-first century, or an East Asian or Latin American, should cause you no difficulty. If you are coming from any of a number of other cultures, however, you might need quite a bit of guidance. I will assume that you, my reader (patient friend, I think of you often), do not. As a poem about baseball (or softball) pitching the poem is quite accurate. I used to pitch myself, half a century ago, and I know very well what goes through a pitcher's mind. To avoid the obvious and vary the avoidance — yes, watch someone like Pedro Martinez or his brother Ramon and you will see the process in practice. It is a disaster for a pitcher to be "wild," but it is necessary that the pitcher be unpredictable: "seeming aberration willed," that's the ticket. The fastball up and in, followed once by the curve outside and next time by another inside fastball. Yes. We situate the poem by clothing its abstractions in specifics. As a poem about pitching, I like it. I like it personally. It wakes memories of hours on the mound, of youthful joys and sorrows, and it informs my present occasions of watching the sport. But there is something else going on here, something that catches the attentive eye of the crafty reader.

Consider some of the words used that do not come from the world of the diamond: *comprehended, misunder-*

stood, communicate, understand. All these words have to do with language and meaning, and there are other phrases in the poem, like "avoid the obvious," which works as well with reference to language as it does with reference to baseball. There is a pattern here. The poet/speaker is talking about baseball, for sure, but he may be talking about something else as well. We are in the area of the "symbol" and the secret-hidden-deeper-meaning, here, and must move cautiously. There is no secret, nothing hidden. But there may well be a delayed meaning, a meaning meant to appear plainly only after the reader has swung at it and missed or taken it for a called strike. All these references to language and meaning indicate that the poet may be talking about a way of communicating. He talks about two ways of throwing: "The others throw to be comprehended. He / Throws to be a moment misunderstood." On the baseball field eight players throw the ball as straight as they can, intending that somebody should catch it with as little trouble as possible. They do not always succeed in this — ask any first baseman about it. But they do not deliberately throw curves or sinkers to one another. Only the pitcher does this. But all those words that point toward language and meaning invite us to look for an analogy between the baseball situation and something in the world of communication.

The crafty reader will not be long in formulating the problem this way: pitcher : fielders :: X : other communicators. From here how long can it take such a reader to reach X = Poet? Or, finally pitcher : fielders :: poet : prose writers. A definition of poetry is being proposed here. Francis is arguing that the meaning of a poem should be clear enough, but not immediately. It should involve a "moment" of misunderstanding, followed by comprehension that comes "too late." In this formulation the reader is like a batter with two strikes on him, frozen by a slow curve that breaks over the plate. And the poem tries to enact precisely that process, freezing us into reading it as a poem about baseball only, only to discover, too late, that it is a poem about poetry as well. Which means that it is about a third thing, the relation between the art of pitching and the ars poetica. The poem practices what it preaches, in more ways than one. Look at the rhymes, or rather look for the rhymes: aim/ aim at, avoid/avoidance, He/be —, wild/willed, communicate/late. They don't all come at the end of the lines and they are not exact. Sometimes they are repetitions of the same syllable but in different locations. Only the last rhyme is what we expect — and by then we don't expect it. "His technique how to vary" — indeed — and how well the word *technique* fits both poet and pitcher!

This is a clever poem — and it is clever in a rather New Critical way. That is, it points to a kind of poetry that fits nicely into that way of reading. I think a full response to this poem would be to ask whether there are other ways of pitching and other kinds of poems. Aren't there baseball pitchers and softball pitchers who just keep throwing that high hard one or that screaming sinker and daring the batter to catch up with it? Could there be poets who do the same thing? What would be the poetical equivalent of a 95 mph fastball? Maybe the analogy breaks down if you push it too hard. Maybe the poem is really talking about only one kind of pitcher and one kind of poet. But the poem is a pleasure to read and think about. And if you like it, it will stick in your head.

It has no secret meanings, no symbols. It wants "still, still to communicate." Just not too fast, not too simply. Poems often want to slow up the process of comprehension a bit. They want to encourage second and third readings. They want to stick in your head, to stimulate thoughts and feelings. A crafty reader will pick up the pattern that leads to a second set of meanings and follow that pattern with pleasure. To think and feel in this way is to be more alive — not the only way, to be sure, for reading about pitching is not the same as pitching any more than reading about love is the same as making it. But these things sometimes touch, as in the case of Paolo and Francesca in Dante, Swann and Odette in Proust.

We develop our craft as readers of poetry by reading poems, thinking about them, talking about them. That is why a textbook can carry so much weight. A good curator in an art gallery can often teach viewers something important simply by putting together two pictures for them to consider in relation to each other. There are many ways to combine poems for instructive purposes. Something as obvious as printing Robert Francis's poem "Catch" next to his poem "Pitcher" might be quite useful. Here I want to bring together three poems that use almost the same situation and seem to be saying almost the same thing, to see what we can learn about the craft of reading poetry by comparing them. I shall start with two and bring the third one in later.

Song of a Second April

April, this year, not otherwise
    Than April of a year ago,

Is full of whispers, full of sighs,
Of dazzling mud and dingy snow;
Hepaticas that pleased you so
Are here again, and butterflies.

There rings a hammering all day,
And shingles lie about the doors;
In orchards near and far away
The grey wood-pecker taps and bores;
And men are merry at their chores,
And children earnest at their play.

The larger streams run still and deep,
Noisy and swift the small brooks run
Among the mullein stalks the sheep
Go up the hillside in the sun,
Pensively, — only you are gone,
You that alone I cared to keep.

This is a simple poem based on the difference between last April and this "second April," in which everything is "not otherwise" than last year, except that a beloved person, addressed directly as "You" in the poem, is missing. And here is another, by a different poet, describing a very similar situation:

I so liked Spring

I so liked Spring last year
Because you were here; —
The thrushes too —
Because it was these you so liked to hear —
I so liked you.

This year's a different thing. —
　　I'll not think of you.
But I'll like Spring because it is simply
　Spring
　　　As the thrushes do.

Once again, we have last year and this year, in spring, marked by the repetition of natural things (in this case represented only by the thrushes) and the absence of a beloved called "you." Both poems are based upon the contrast between the repetition of the annual cycle of nature and the changing temporality of the human world. They speak to us of the fragility of human relationships, of what it feels like to be in a season, a time-place, once shared with a beloved person and now marked by that person's absence. This is what Roland Barthes called a "scene of language," a common experience already written, as it were, but always in need of rewriting, so that we who experience the absence of a once-beloved person can recognize that this experience is not unique to us, however it may feel, but something shared by others, a common kind of pain, which is assuaged, as Beckett hinted, by the words that are applied to it.

We may say that these poems are "touching" or "sentimental," if not "sensational"—the material out of which soap operas are made. They differ from actual soaps mainly in their brevity, and in the ways they connect the personal experience of the speakers to other concerns, human and natural. But this is not a different order of textual experience or pleasure from what we may find in the popular media. The connection that Brooks and Warren mentioned but did not provide, between poetry and television, is not difficult to find. It is already there — in the poems themselves. But the poems must be read — by readers — for themselves. This apparently simple proposition contradicts the critical method at the core of the New Criticism — which is still alive and well in the work of Harold Bloom today — in which the critic or teacher reads the poem on behalf of others. As the New Critic W. K. Wimsatt put it in his essay on "The Affective Fallacy," "The critic is . . . a teacher or explicator of meanings" (Wimsatt 34). In Wimsatt's view the critic or teacher performs the explication on behalf of other readers or students. This is not so much teaching a craft or method as it is impressing the audience with the art of the explicator, explication becoming, in this way, a sort of secondary art, and the teacher or explicator a sort of artist — or, if not an artist, a priestly exegete. Wimsatt's book is not called *The Verbal Icon* for nothing. And it ends, let us not forget, with an essay on "Poetry and Christianity," in which he quotes approvingly a British Dominican father who said that "good writing is a part of truth. If you take a true proposition and state it in a sentimental way, in a sectarian way, in a vulgar way, you damage the truth of it" (Wimsatt 277). I am arguing that, by pushing poetry too far, raising it too high — to the level of truth, to a level of inhuman purity — the New Critics made a great error in a worthy cause. Wimsatt himself was aware of this possibility, and acknowledged that "there is such a thing as art which is pure and at the same time sickly, mawkish, tawdry, or fraudulent" (277), but this is only to repeat the notion that vulgarity can contaminate truth. My point is that by positioning the critic or teacher as mainly an explicator, the objects of explication — poems, little arrangements of words —

were forced into an impossibly high status. Poems had to become icons to be worthy of the explicator's art.

If, on the other hand, we can allow poems to be less exalted yet still worthy of our attention, then it should be possible to speak of a craft of reading poetry that can be mastered by ordinary readers. Using the two poems quoted above, I should like to continue my demonstration of the rudiments of such a craft, elaborating a bit further some of the procedures outlined above. We can begin by returning to those phrases belatedly inserted in the introduction to *Understanding Poetry*, reminding us "that the poet is a man speaking to men, and that every poem is, at center, a little drama." Dropping the distracting reference to gender, these two notions offer a useful way into the craft of reading. A poem is an utterance from a poet to us, the poem's readers. And it is also, often, a little drama, which means that the speaker may be understood as playing a role, as a character in a certain situation. A little space opens up here, potentially, between the poet who writes and the character who speaks the lines. If the distance opens to a perceptible gap, we are likely to be in the presence of irony, which the New Critics admired, rightly, though perhaps excessively. We will seldom go wrong, however, in reading a poem, if we begin by inquiring about the speaker and the dramatic situation of the spoken words. But we should also notice that by insisting that *every* poem must be a drama, the New Critics excluded poems that are, say, little essays, addressing the reader directly, as Millay does in her "Justice Denied" and as Robert Francis did in "Pitcher," which is an essay/poem on the craft of pitching.

W. K. Wimsatt follows the "poetry as little drama" line in his introduction to *The Verbal Icon*, citing with approval "the often quoted statement by J. S. Mill that 'Eloquence is *heard*, poetry is *over*-heard'" (Wimsatt 15), which is another version of the rhetoric/poetics opposition so crucial to modernist critical thought. As we have seen, however, some poems are heard and others overheard. Some poems are more like essays, others more like plays or stories. Poetry is thus not a genre but a delivery system, something resembling a medium, within which we will find a number of genres. The fundamental New Critical error is to treat it as a genre of supreme purity, cut off from other kinds of texts and the experiences embodied in them. My aim here is to save what is useful in the New Criticism while discarding those features of New Critical doctrine that have worked to separate poetry from other kinds of textual experience. In this connection a revealing discussion may be found in Wimsatt's essay "The Concrete Universal." At a certain point he introduces the name of Edgar Guest as the author of "newspaper poems" that lack "artistic unity." Not surprising, you may say, but then comes a footnote. In this note Wimsatt says that a reader he esteems has complained that Guest's name should not even be uttered in a serious discussion of poetry, that "such a name appears in a serious discussion of poetics anomalously and in bad taste." Wimsatt then asserts that he has kept the name because he wants to insist on the existence of "badness" in poetry as a point of reference for talking about "goodness," and he explicitly rejects such euphemisms as "mediocrity." A couple of things about this textual moment are interesting. One is that it reveals a climate of thought in which the very name of the author of such lines as "It takes a heap o' livin' in a house t' make it home" is anathema, almost like uttering a religious blasphemy. And another is that the elimination of a poetic middle ground (mediocrity) was a deliberate part of the New Critical program. (By the way, this line, which is often stitched into moral fabrics, is usually misquoted on them. But you can find the full correct text on the Web, easily.)

In another essay Wimsatt cites approvingly Tate's attempt in "Tension in Poetry" to provide a philosophical basis for badness in certain romantic and metaphysical poems. But in the craft of reading poetry there is no need to ground poetic appreciation in a rejection of badness. The lover of Edgar Guest is not wrong to love him, in my judgment, and the line I quoted is both memorable and true enough to be worth remembering. Moreover, there is reason to hope that a lover of Edgar Guest may learn to love other kinds of poems — but not if some teacher starts off by trashing the beloved poet and his work. One might wish to put next to Guest's line about home Robert Frost's mordant "Home is the place where, when you have to go there, / They have to take you in" (from "Death of the Hired Man"), but Frost does not erase or nullify Guest. Taken together the two phrases open the way to a discussion about what is involved in the notion of "home." In both cases, of course, we will get further if we look at the whole poems involved and ask about who is speaking those words. In Frost's poem the words are in fact uttered in a discussion between a husband and wife about "what you mean by home."

The two poems about spring quoted above will take us a bit deeper into the craft of reading poetry, if we begin with questions about the speakers and their situations. The situations of the two poems, and the speakers' responses to them, upon closer examination are rather different. That is, each poem offers a different way of dealing with the common experience. The first is a cry of pain, the second a resolve to be more like the creatures of nature, and "not think" about the "you," whose absence dominates the poem. Let me try to suggest how aspects of the craft of reading poetry might be picked up by means of a discussion of the two poems. If this were happening in a classroom, the teacher would be mindful that the goal of the discussion was neither the explication of the poems nor their evaluation, though both of those matters might have a role to play. The goal would be what the discussants could learn about the craft of reading, and this would be better picked up indirectly than insisted upon dogmatically.

One might begin by asking not about the absolute goodness or badness of the poems but about which is more moving, more interesting, more pleasurable? If I were discussing these poems with a class, instead of just throwing a few hasty words in their direction near the end of a long essay, I would want to explore with my students both their responses to the two poems and the ways we all must deal with this kind of experience, along with the way in which each poem's speaker seems to be dealing with it. And I would encourage them to work out the differences in each situation to the extent that the clues in the poems allow this to be done. I would even go so far as to encourage research into the lives of these poets — the first poem was written by Edna St. Vincent Millay (80), the second by Charlotte Mew (48) — to see whether or not these anonymous "speakers" might or might not just happen to be speaking of their authors' own situations. I should do this, of course, with a nod to Odette de Crécy and her author, Marcel Proust.

I would also encourage my students to compose poems that appropriate either the situation or the formal features of these poems — or both — for one of the best responses to a poem is surely another poem. In discussing a poem or imitating one, we soon discover the need for terms to describe what we are seeing and doing. This is the point where technical vocabulary can best be introduced. It will be important here to note how regular Millay's rhythm is, and how much closer to ordinary speech is Mew's. But these two particular poems get most of their power from the dramatic situation, in which two scenes are superimposed upon each other, with a central character present in the absent scene and absent in the present one. Understanding how that little trick is worked will be one of the rewards for looking carefully at the two poems. But the main reward must lie in the way that they express emotions that we recognize as our own, in response to situations in which we have all surely found ourselves at one time or another and will find ourselves again. A learned friend of mine tells me that there is a topos in Arabic poetry in which the poet comes to an oasis where something happened years before and muses upon the past and the present. Poetry may not be quite universal, but poetic effects and procedures do indeed range across the cultures.

There are many nice little touches in both poems, felicities of sound and thought, like the men who are merry at work and the children who are earnest at play in Millay's poem — not obvious but just right — and the way that the speaker's affection for "you" in Mew's poem is so nicely entangled with the way "you" responded to the thrushes — as in Millay's with the hepaticas. The economy of means in relation to effect, so conspicuous in

Mew's treatment, is also admirable. (Even Allen Tate might have admired it, I like to think.) These poems were written around the same time, close to 1920, and Millay's was published first, though Mew's may have been written earlier. Millay loved men, mostly, and Mew women. Does this make a difference? Or is love just love? Wanting to know more about the lives of these poets seems to be a reasonable and proper response to poetry, as it did to Samuel Johnson when he wrote *The Lives of the Poets* so many years ago. The clues in both poems tease us into thought about the situations and relations that are adumbrated there. What has happened? Death? Separation? Or the breaking of what was once a strong emotional tie, the end of some kind of affair? If many poems are "little dramas," in Brooks and Warren's words, often there are pieces of the drama missing, and the craft of reading poetry involves the ability to supply those pieces in a way that completes the dramatic situation sketched by the poet without doing violence to the evidence provided.

But what about judgment? Is there a place for it in the craft of reading? Indeed yes, though I would want that place to be a forum rather than a pulpit. Personally, I think that Millay's poem is finally not quite as interesting as Mew's, because her oppositions (playful workers, serious children) are a bit too formulaic (along with the dazzling mud and dingy snow). That is, these things are mere reversals of the obvious expectation (playful children, serious workers, dazzling snow, dingy mud). I grant that there is a rightness to them, but the repetition of the device takes away from its effectiveness, in my judgment. I also feel that the cry in Millay's last line ("You, that I would have kept") is such an obvious ap-

peal for sympathy that I am inclined to resist it. Whereas
Mew's stiff upper lip brings out my sympathy with a
rush. I fear, of course, that the New Critics would join me
in this appraisal. That is, I fear that what I learned from
them is indeed important to me personally and to the kind
of craft of reading that I would like to teach. It has gone so
deep, in fact, that I must work constantly to undo its effects. Which I do, my crafty readers, which I do.

Let us now complicate things by looking at a third
poem in the same vein:

Spring

To what purpose, April, do you return again?
Beauty is not enough.
You can no longer quiet me with redness
Of little leaves opening stickily.
I know what I know.
The sun is hot on my neck as I observe
The spikes of the crocus.
The smell of the earth is good.
It is apparent that there is no death.
But what does that signify?
Not only under ground are the brains of men
Eaten by maggots.
Life in itself
Is nothing.
An empty cup, a flight of uncarpeted stairs.
It is not enough that yearly, down this hill,
April
Comes like an idiot, babbling and strewing
    flowers.

If this were a course, I might simply throw that poem by Edna Millay (Millay 53) at my students, pointing out that it is from the same volume of verse as Millay's other April poem, the volume called *Second April,* and ask them to discuss the two poems. But here I must do some of that work myself. In that volume one of the two Millay April poems, obviously, bears the book's title. The other, "Spring," however, appears first in the volume, in italic type which sets it apart from the rest. Both poems are given special importance, then, by the way the author has used them and placed them. For our purposes, however, what is important is the way the two poems resemble each other and yet are very different. This poem, for example, is written in free verse, without rhyme, and with the spacing of words carrying a good deal of weight, as in the isolation of the word *April* in the next-to-last line, which leads the reader to emphasize the word, perhaps in a tone of exasperation. It seems to me that Millay, who has great facility with rhythm and rhyme, does best when she does not rely on this too heavily, as in "Spring."

But there are other interesting things about this poem in comparison with "Second April." Both are April poems, but this one expresses a very different emotion. Though it starts by addressing the month as if it were a person, it ends by talking about April in the third person — as an idiot who comes babbling and strewing flowers. This is a kind of metaphysical conceit. We remember that John Donne called the sun a "busy old fool" for shining upon him and his lover in bed and driving them out of it. The New Critics, who find this tolerable or even admirable in Donne, find this sort of thing "unintelligible" when Millay does it. In this case, however, the in-

congruity between April's careless beauties and some
care or burden is clear enough — but just what the care
or burden may be is far less clear. The speaker/poet says
ominously, "I know what I know." But what she knows
in this case is not death or separation. "It is apparent that
there is no death," she says — a line that will bear some
thought and discussion. To understand it we shall have
to follow that thought for a few lines to its conclusion,
which turns on the notion that the brains of men may be
eaten by maggots while the men are alive and above
ground. The metaphor here, which approaches the
metaphysical or perhaps the surreal, must be read — like
Herrick's numbering of Jone's few hairs — as an ironic
exaggeration. Presumably a brain devoured by maggots
would not function well. Somebody has done something
stupid and the poet is really angry about it — that is what
these lines suggest. This is an emotion we must all share
at one time or another. (Let me tell you about the minds
of academic administrators — but no, this is not the
place.) Because we don't know the cause, however, we
cannot judge the justice of this emotion. We may wish to
see it as a kind of venting of rage, an excess that has a
touch of the comic in it. That complaint against poor innocent April, after all, is a bit much, as is John Donne's
complaint about the sun. If we see it that way — and I am
only proposing this as a possibility, you understand —
then we may see our own emotions as sometimes excessive, though the need to vent or express them may be
very great.

A poem like this should be an occasion for sharing
tales of things that have made us that angry, for this is a
poem of anger rather than anguish, and poetry is meant
to be a vehicle that helps to break down the barriers that

often prevent us from speaking to one another about our feelings. Just as we like to go to a concert or a play or a film or an art gallery with someone so that we can talk over what we have seen or heard, we should like poetry for the same reason, because it provides us with potent objects for conversation, objects that mediate between one human being and another, encouraging us to communicate more fully. And some poems are indeed funny, while others may be sentimental. Millay is often close to the sentimental, which makes her a real test case for the New Critics, who so despised sentimentality. But what is sentimentality, anyway? Keeping it simple, I should say that we are inclined to put that label on any text that appeals strongly for an emotional response of the sympathetic sort, with the implication usually being that the appeal is in excess of what the situation calls for, or — and this is the interesting part — in excess of what the language of the appealer is able to evoke. Millay is skillful with language, but she also goes for strong emotions. Mew, in her April poem, played it safe by understating the emotion. Millay, in both of hers, plays it anything but safe. She pours out her sorrow or her anger — and the New Critics recoil in horror.

In my personal judgment, Millay is not Emily Dickinson (who is?), but she is far too good a poet to lose, and an excellent poet to study and discuss. The New Critics, of course, by insisting on the highest standard, and defining that in terms of order and control, denied her the status of "good poet" and, having no category of "slightly less good" or "pretty good," consigned her to oblivion with Edgar Guest, the "newspaper poet," and all the others whose work was supposed to be "bad." You won't find much of Walt Whitman in *Understanding*

Poetry, either, and for similar reasons. These are poets who pour out the emotion, constantly risk sentimentality, and tackle subjects that are social and political as well as those that are perhaps too personal for comfort. All of this makes Allen Tate's New Critical attack on Millay's "Justice Denied in Massachusetts" especially important. It is a poem of a sort that the New Critics can scarcely admit to be poetry — a poem of social protest. It is also one of her strongest poems. If Tate was right about that poem, then they may well have been right about her work in general and justified in ignoring it. Do I think they were right? Not for a minute. But let us look at the poem — the whole poem — and let us situate it in its proper context:

Justice Denied in Massachusetts

Let us abandon then our gardens and go
    home
And sit in the sitting-room.
Shall the larkspur blossom or the corn grow
    under this cloud?
Sour to the fruitful seed
Is the cold earth under this cloud,
Fostering quack and weed, we have marched
    upon but cannot conquer;
We have bent the blades of our hoes against
    the stalks of them.

Let us go home, and sit in the sitting-room.
Not in our day
Shall the cloud go over and the sun rise as be-
    fore,

Beneficent upon us
Out of the glittering bay,
And the warm winds be blown inward from
    the sea
Upon the blades of corn
With a peaceful sound.
Forlorn, forlorn,
Stands the blue hay-rack by the empty mow,
And the petals drop to the ground,
Leaving the tree unfruited.
The sun that warmed our stooping backs and
    withered the weed uprooted —
We shall not feel it again.
We shall die in darkness and be buried in the
    rain.

What from the splendid dead
We have inherited —
Furrows sweet to the grain, and the weed
    subdued —
See now the slug and the mildew plunder,
Evil does overwhelm
The larkspur and the corn;
We have seen them go under.

Let us sit here, sit still,
Here in the sitting-room until we die;
At the step of Death on the walk, rise and go;
Leaving to our children's children this beau-
    tiful doorway,
And this elm,
And a blighted earth to till
With a broken hoe.

Situate, situate. The title does a lot to locate us. This is a poem about a particular injustice in Massachusetts — or that is what it claims. But this is only a clue. The crafty reader must follow it up. And we shall do that, but first let us look at the text that is before us, and situate the speaker and those addressed. The speaker addresses an "us" in the first line, but I don't think that this is primarily you and me. This is a local us and the time is an immediate "then." T. S. Eliot, who also wrote about Massachusetts occasionally, once began a poem (since become famous) with the words, "Let us go then . . . " Millay begins with, "Let us abandon then our gardens . . . " The echo of Eliot may or may not be intentional, but Eliot's poem is about going out on a visit, while Millay's is about going home to sit. The literal sense of Millay's poem is not difficult to glean. We (she and her fellows, in this case apparently her fellow citizens of Massachusetts) should stop cultivating the earth, abandon their gardens, and go sit, sit still, in the room they refer to as the sitting room. They should do this, she says, because the earth is blighted. Nothing will grow there any more, because a cloud — "this cloud" — has come over the earth and will not go away in the time of the present generation.

This is plain enough, I should think. And a large part of the craft of a crafty reader of poetry is simply to pay attention to plain things, to notice them and not let them slip by. The meaning in poetry is not hidden mysteriously but can be got at just by paying attention. But back to the poem. A cloud that will not go away is a strange phenomenon, like something out of science fiction or the plagues of Egypt in the Bible. It should be enough to drive the crafty reader off the literal level of meaning — but we don't leave that level without a cause. In this case our craft should suggest a connection between the strange behavior of this cloud, the moment ("then") mentioned in the first line, and the poem's title. The cause of the cloud has something to do with "justice denied"; the moment is the moment of denial; and the people addressed are the citizens of the place where justice has been denied — Massachusetts — a place where the sun should rise,

> Beneficent upon us
> Out of the glittering bay,
> And the warm winds be blown inward from
>   the sea
> Upon the blades of corn
> With a peaceful sound.

In "The Bay State" that is just the way things normally work. That is, Millay is giving a geographically correct picture of the place and its weather. She is also tinting that picture with words that connote beauty and joy. But none of this is mysterious or even difficult for a crafty reader.

The poem also speaks historically, about "the splendid dead" from whom the living have inherited the fruitful land. Who are these dead, at whom Allen Tate sneered gratuitously ("her splendid ancestors")? In Massachusetts they are called patriots — which is why their professional football team bears that name — and they are so called because they led a successful revolution against England in the name of justice. They had names like Adams and Hancock. Again, none of this is difficult to discover. Tate professed to be puzzled at "how Massachusetts could cause a general desiccation"—but this is a willful misreading of the text. Millay never says that Massachusetts caused anything, nor that the desiccation is general. She says that the denial of justice caused a desiccation in Massachusetts, where justice had once flourished but was now denied. Again, this should be plain to a reader crafty enough to read plainly, paying attention to what is being said. But we haven't yet considered the occasion, the specific nature of this denial of justice. We know that there is not a real cloud sitting permanently over Massachusetts, because we know that nature doesn't work that way. We know, also, that this metaphorical cloud has something to do with what the poet considered to be a denial of justice—a denial especially unworthy of a state and a country founded on resistance to injustice. We also know, because Allen Tate told us, that the particular injustice she had in mind was the trial and subsequent electrocution of two Italian-Americans, Nicola Sacco and Bartolomeo Vanzetti. Tate tells us that he learned this from a footnote. Is this proper? Should a poem need notes? Perhaps we should ask T. S. Eliot. But let us take those questions seriously. How should this poem be presented in a textbook, in an anthology, in a curriculum, in a classroom?

It is an occasional poem—a poem tied to a specific event. The crafty reader will want to know something about that event and the poem's connection to it. Run the words "Sacco and Vanzetti" through any search engine on the Web, and you will get a good deal of information about the trial, the execution, and the aftermath. But the poem will read best if we situate it in its original setting, in a collection of poems edited by Lucia Trent and Ralph

Cheney and published in 1928 as *America Arraigned!* After a foreword by the editors and an introduction by John Haynes Holmes, the book is organized into sections of poems written at different stages in the process of trial and execution. Some of the poems were written before the electrocution, when there was still hope that the governor of Massachusetts, or even President Coolidge, might stay the death sentence. If I were putting Millay's poem in a book or teaching it in a course, I would want the following passage from the foreword to be included:

> Before August 23rd, 1927, day of eternal shame to America, we sent part of the manuscript of this book to Sacco and Vanzetti and to Gov. Alvin T. Fuller accompanied by the following letter to the governor:
>
>> In the name of the foremost poets of America we are sending you part of the manuscript of an anthology of poems protesting again the conviction and punishment of Sacco and Vanzetti, which will be published in the event that these men are not set free. These poems are an indication of the attitude of our poets in regard to this case. If these innocent martyrs are sent to the chair or to prison as victims of war hysteria, and every prejudice and force opposed to civilization, this book will live to cry shame on the justice of Massachusetts.
>> Yours for American fair play.
>
> (Trent 9)

The sections of the book have these titles:

- BEFORE GOVERNOR FULLER AND HIS ADVISORY COMMISSION REFUSED TO INTERCEDE

- AFTER INTERCESSION WAS REFUSED BUT BEFORE THE CRUCIFIXION

- AFTER THE CRUCIFIXION

Millay's poem is in the third section of the book. Among the nearly sixty poems in the collection it stands out as a well-crafted, orderly poem. It does not make the easy connection to the passion of Christ that is used by the editors and many of the writers, not does it make far-fetched allusions to Greek tragedy, as one of the editors does in a prose poem about meeting Vanzetti's daughter in Paris. It is built around a single image, as we have noted, the image of a cloud covering Massachusetts and turning it into an infertile waste land. But where did the cloud come from? We can simply take it as a metaphor, but I believe it is a metaphor grounded in the actual situation. In his poem, which appears a few pages after Millay's in the anthology, John Dos Passos wrote:

> They are dead now
> The black automatons have won.
> They are burned up utterly
> their flesh has passed into the air of Massa-
> chusetts
> . . . .
> so they are dead now and burned
> into the fierce wind from Massachusetts.

Their breath has given the wind new speed.
Their fire has burned out of the wind
the stale smell of Boston. (82–83)

The burning in Dos Passos's poem is not simply a metaphor. It is a way — an ordinary way — of talking about death in the electric chair. In his impassioned introduction to this anthology John Haynes Holmes speaks of the night of August 22, 1927, as the night on which Sacco and Vanzetti "were burned to death in the electric chair" (15). But burning in this instance has a second, more literal significance. The bodies of the two men were cremated. John Dos Passos took these "burnings" and read them in a way that combined the metaphorical with the literal: "their flesh has passed into the air of Massachusetts." Whatever is burned will in fact pass into the air. Millay used a similar notion, adding to it the common metaphor of a shadow or cloud used to express gloom or sorrow. And then she worked out, quite literally, some of the things that might be caused by a perpetual cloud over farmland, just as she took the common term *sitting room* and, by harping on *sit* and *sitting,* generated a notion of helpless inactivity. Allen Tate, for reasons of his own, pretended to find all this unintelligible and argued that it was the disordered work of mass language in action. I am arguing that it is indeed drawn from common language but is highly ordered and clearly intelligible. It is very much a poem about a great state with a proud heritage of patriotism and justice, a state that had used its power to kill legally — a power reserved to the states and the federal government in this country — in a way that Millay and others believed had brought shame on that proud heritage — "what from the splendid dead / We have inherited."

It is a somber poem and the form Millay uses is somber. In "Second April" she used a very regular sort of rhythm and rhyme. One could even argue that it is too bouncy for the meaning. But in "Justice Denied" she uses the structure of a formal ode (a notion the crafty reader picks up from reading a lot of poems in different forms). The lines are irregular in length. The rhymes come at irregular intervals, and many of them are off-rhymes or not-quite-rhymes like "bay" and "sea," or "home" and "room." Some lines use the oldest device in English poetry, alliteration, as a way of tying their words together ("garden . . . grow," "Sour . . . seed," "bent . . . blades," "warm winds . . . in*ward*," "warmed . . . withered . . . weed," "die . . . darkness"). Though it is a public poem, a poem of protest, written for an occasion, using a common language and a simple metaphor, it is not any of those things that Allen Tate accused it of being: a poem of sentimental emotion in mass language "achieved, as it is here, without conscious effort." There are other poems in *America Arraigned!* that seem well done to me, and many that might be justly accused of excesses of disordered feeling. It would be useful, I think, to collect a number of these poems and discuss their strengths and weaknesses. It would be a way for readers to improve their craft. In such a collection I would certainly include Vanzetti's words to the judge who condemned him, as quoted in the introduction by John Haynes Holmes:

If it had not been for these things, I might have live out my life, talking at street-

corners to scorning men. I might have die, un-
marked, unknown, a failure. Now we are not
a failure. This is our career and our triumph.
Never in our full life can we hope to do much
work for tolerance, for justice, for man's understanding of man, as now we do by an accident. Our words, our lives, our pains — nothing! The taking of our lives — lives of a good
shoemaker and a poor fish-peddler — all!
That last moment belong to us — that agony is
our triumph! (16)

Whatever else he was, Bartolomeo Vanzetti was a poet.
Certainly, there is no poem in the collection any more effective than this. Without complete control of the grammar of this foreign language, Vanzetti still made it his
own. Is this mass language? John Holmes called these
words "immortal," which is a lot to say about any words,
but they have lived and will live for some time, with
every ungrammaticality cherished. They show, among
other things, that poetry doesn't have to be in verse. This
is poetry, however, in the way that it compresses so much
of life into a phrase like "talking at street-corners to
scorning men" — an image that embodies all those who
preach idealistic gospels in a materialistic culture. Anar-
chism never looked so good as it does in Vanzetti's
words — and this is partly because the words recognize
the futility of words themselves, of "talking." The anar-
chists believed in the propaganda of the deed, and that is
the language Vanzetti is putting into words, because, as
it turns out, words and deeds need one another.

My case against the New Criticism is that it opened
up too great a space between words and deeds, and be-

tween the rhetorical and the poetic. It took a certain patrician attitude of cool detachment and made it the measure of all good writing. And it developed a method of reading, an art of reading poetry, that emphasized the technical qualities of form over the human qualities of expression. Their art of reading poetry was superb, in all senses of that word, but now it is time for schools and teachers to offer instruction in a more humble craft of reading poetry. We have nothing to lose but our tensions.

Reading the World

Textual Realities

Learning is essentially concerned with *signs*. Signs are the object of a temporal apprenticeship, not of an abstract knowledge. To learn is first of all to consider a substance, an object, a being as if they emitted signs to be deciphered, interpreted. . . . One becomes a carpenter only by becoming sensitive to the signs of wood, a physician by becoming sensitive to the signs of disease. Vocation is always predestination with regard to signs. Everything which teaches us something emits signs, every act of learning is an interpretation of signs.

Gilles Deleuze

We live in a textual reality. One does not have to be a French philosopher to know this. Most young people know it, whether they are fully conscious of this knowledge or not. And most of their elders know it, whether they care to admit it or not. On this occasion I want to explore with you some of the implications of this knowledge. But first, I must try to explain just what I mean by "textual reality" — and what I do not mean. Let me start with the negative: what I do not mean. I am not trying to suggest that if you cut yourself you will not bleed. Shakespeare's Shylock used this very notion in trying to get his Christian neighbors to acknowledge his humanity: Jews bleed, he argued, therefore they are as human — and as real — as the other inhabitants of Venice. And, of course, Shylock was forced to consider just that point in court, when he was ordered to take his pound of flesh without drawing blood. The connection of flesh and blood is not merely textual, however powerfully textualized by Shakespeare. Nor am I suggesting that there is anything unreal, or merely textual, about our pain and suffering, or about what we endure as human beings. I have watched the mortal remains of a beloved son go trundling down the ramp into the furnace of a cut-rate crematorium. I have lost a part of my hearing while "defending democracy" off the coast of Korea. These things are real, they are irreversible, they are not *merely* textual. What happens to each of us happens to us alone. As Blaise Pascal observed in a powerful text, "one will die alone." That each of us will indeed die — that is scripted, though the details are hidden in the contingent future. That we will do it alone — that is also scripted, once by the "conditions of being in which we find ourselves," as Beckett put it (81), and again in Pascal's words, a text which, if we use it rightly, will help us face those very conditions.

Texts, I am suggesting, give meaning even to the contingent and fleeting events of our ordinary lives, and that is one reason why we value them. But the conditions of our being come to us already scripted, textualized, shaped in patterns into which we fall, almost like actors given a script that they must follow. The human condition is a condition of textuality. What I hope to accomplish here is to follow this trail for a bit, looking at instances of textualization and varieties of textual reality, and then conclude by considering the pedagogical implications of our textual condition.

Textuality runs deep, since all human beings can be seen as textual animals in more than one sense. First of all, like every other living thing, we replicate ourselves through the transmission of genetic information coded in the nucleonic acids, DNA and RNA. We are, biologically, the result of a textual process. We have been scripted. Beyond that, of course, human beings are born into linguistic and cultural heritages that are themselves powerful texts, shaping our possibilities and impossibilities, and we function amid webs of information carried by various audible, visual, and verbal media that shape the ways we live and die. We never escape textuality, and if we live after death, it will be textually, in signs — memories, photographs, words in pixels or on a page or cut into stone.

The human condition, then, is a textual condition, and has always been so. I thought of this the other day when I was reading a column by Dave Barry in which he said that he is hospitable to all religions, "because you never know." And he went on to imagine arriving at the pearly gates and being greeted there by L. Ron Hubbard, the founder of the Church of Scientology. Pascal thought it made sense to bet that there was a God. Barry suggests going a step further and covering all the numbers on the board. But L. Ron Hubbard visited me by way of Barry's text just in time to help me clarify what I mean by a textual reality. Before he founded his new religion, of course, Hubbard wrote some amusing science fiction novels and stories. One that I remember, written about fifty years ago, was called *Typewriter in the Sky*. In it a man to whom strange things keep happening wonders why this is so, and why he sometimes hears a sound like a great typewriter in the sky. It turns out that he is a character in a novel, whose life is actually being typewritten by the author. This, however, is not exactly what I mean.

None of us lives a life entirely controlled by an outside force in this way. But much of what happens to us in life falls into patterns that are already there, in the culture, waiting for us. This process was represented persuasively by Roland Barthes in his book *Fragments of a Lover's Discourse*, in which Barthes showed how, when we say we "fall in love," we are actually falling into a system of "figures" — scenes and situations that have been textualized before. "Figures take shape," Barthes said, "insofar as we can recognize, in passing discourse, something that has been read, heard, felt. The figure is outlined (like a sign) and memorable (like an image or tale). A figure is established whenever someone can say: *"That's so true! I recognize that scene of language"* (Barthes 4 [modified]). Every love story is different, but each one contains many of the same elements, already written figures such as the *avowal* (the act of saying "I love you"), the *will to possess*, the lover's *jealousy*, and the couple's recollection of special objects or events, *souvenirs*. These figures are already there, as aspects of our textual reality, waiting for us to inhabit them — and to recognize them as true because they are "scenes of language," events scripted in a code that is already known.

What we call realism, then, in literary works may be nothing more than a reading of those "scenes of language" that shape the actual world and turn its inhabitants into characters upon a textual stage. That is, literary realism may be most real when it represents events that are already "scenes of language." Those stages or "stations" on the via dolorosa of love identified by Roland Barthes had been identified previously in the many works of literature he cites, and especially in Proust's elaborate anatomy of love in his *A la recherche du temps perdu*. This textual principle — that we live not in a chaotic world of random events but in a world of figures or cultural codes — is by no means a recent product of ir-responsible Gallic thought. Let us listen, for a moment, to a few sentences by a rock-solid Englishman on the topic of recurring "scenes of language":

> It has always been the practice of those who are desirous to believe themselves made venerable by length of time, to censure the new comers into life, for want of respect to grey hairs and sage experience, for heady confidence in their own understandings, for hasty conclusions upon partial views, for dis-regard of counsels, which their fathers and grandsires are ready to afford them, and a re-bellious impatience of that subordination to which youth is condemned by nature, as nec-essary to its security from evils into which it would be otherwise precipitated, by the rash-ness of passion, and the blindness of igno-rance.
>
> Every old man complains of the growing depravity of the world, of the petulance and insolence of the rising generation. He re-counts the decency and regularity of former times, and celebrates the discipline and sobri-ety of the age in which his youth was passed: a

happy age, which is now no more to be expected, since confusion has broken in upon
the world, and thrown down all the boundaries of civility and reverence. (Johnson,
from *Rambler* No. 50, 164–65)

These words, as their cadences proclaim, were written
nearly two and a half centuries ago, by Samuel Johnson.
But the sentiments expressed translate easily into our
own world's language — indeed, we may find them on
editorial pages almost every week, and hear them at the
commencement ceremonies and alumni reunions of our
colleges every spring. Johnson knew he was discussing a
topos, a recurring rhetorical theme that had, as he says,
"always been the practice" of those who sought to
demonstrate their own wisdom and virtue at the expense
of the young. He spoke only of the past, but he knew that
the topos he described would continue to be employed in
the future. He knew the difference between words and
things, to be sure, and once kicked a stone to demonstrate that the visible world existed, but as the compiler
of one of the first dictionaries of the English language, he
also knew that we live in a textual reality, full of tropes
and traps — scenes of language waiting to inhabit our
thoughts and direct our tongues.

We may wish to wander freely through our world,
and may even believe that we are doing so, but we always — and sooner rather than later — find the warp and
woof of the cultural text guiding our steps. But there is a
further level of textual reality, the level that Jean Baudrillard has called the "hyperreal." Baudrillard is one of
those French thinkers whose ideas seem at first to be utterly outlandish, absolutely impossible of commanding

our belief — indeed, some of us can scarcely bear to give his thought any attention at all. But then, little by little, we come back to his ideas, and they seem a bit less strange, until we must face the awful possibility that he may be right — if not entirely right, at least partly right. When he suggests, for example, that "when the real is no longer what it used to be, nostalgia assumes its full meaning" (Baudrillard 12), I can visualize Dr. Johnson, in the heaven of lexicographers and semioticians, nodding in agreement. For when Johnson describes his graybeards recalling the world of their youth as a world of "decency and regularity," of "discipline and sobriety," he is putting his pudgy finger squarely on the way nostalgia governs our perceptions of both the past and the present — a present which assumes its shape by way of its supposed difference from earlier times.

Johnson, let us remember, wrote just at the time when what we now call "realism" was moving to the center of the literary stage. He was one of the first to suggest that the recording of an ordinary life would be a valuable undertaking. "I have often thought," he wrote in *Rambler* No. 60 in 1750, "that there has rarely passed a life of which a judicious and faithful narrative would not be useful" (Johnson 168). But he was also acutely aware of the way that human beings moved in textual grooves etched by both culture and what he called "the state of man," saying, "there is such an uniformity in the state of man, considered apart from adventitious and separable decorations and disguises, that there is scarce any possibility for good or ill, but is common to human kind" (Johnson 169). This common quality of human joys and sorrows, as Johnson saw it, did not make life less real. For him the real *was* the common, the general. If reality consists of repeated gestures from an already scripted repertory, then the script itself must be accepted as real. Things look different to us now. Two centuries and more after Johnson, Jean Baudrillard wants to take us further, into a world where everything is so textualized that there is no space left for the real, a world in which we encounter simulations and simulacra at every turn. One of his most telling illustrations of this view begins with a discussion of Disneyland.

> Disneyland is a perfect model of all the entangled orders of simulation. To begin with it is a play of illusions and phantasms: Pirates, the Frontier, Future World, etc. This imaginary world is supposed to be what makes the operation successful. But what draws the crowds is undoubtedly much more the social microcosm, the miniaturized and *religious* revelling in real America, in its delights and drawbacks. You park outside, line up inside, and are totally abandoned at the exit. In this imaginary world the only phantasmagoria is in the inherent warmth and affection of the crowd, and in that sufficiently excessive number of gadgets used there to specifically maintain the multitudinous affect. The contrast with the absolute solitude of the parking lot — a veritable concentration camp — is total. (23–24)

We should notice that Baudrillard is not simply another Frenchman trashing America. He *likes* some of what he sees, and he is quick to notice the "inherent warmth and affection of the crowd" — which seems to me exactly right for the way American crowds behave at festive places and occasions. And I think he is also right about the "religious" quality of this "revelling" in America. He is observing a ritual, and he knows it. But he has more to say, and this is where the real originality of his thought lies. Let us listen to him further:

> Disneyland is there to conceal the fact that it is the "real" country, all of "real" America, which *is* Disneyland. . . . Disneyland is presented as imaginary in order to make us believe that the rest is real, when in fact all of Los Angeles and the America surrounding it are no longer real but of the order of the hyperreal and simulation. . . . [Disneyland] is meant to be an infantile world, in order to make us believe that the adults are elsewhere, in the "real" — and to conceal the fact that real childishness is everywhere. . . .
>
> Moreover, Disneyland is not the only one. Enchanted Village, Magic Mountain, Marine World: Los Angeles is encircled by these "imaginary stations" which feed reality, reality-energy, to a town whose mystery is precisely nothing more than a network of endless, unreal circulation . . . a town which is nothing more than an immense script and a perpetual motion picture. (25–26)

Baudrillard, writing in the early 1980s, went on to discuss the Watergate affair as a scandal generated to conceal the fact that nothing is scandalous any more. It is not difficult to see what he would have made of the Monica

Lewinsky business. If we ever needed evidence of just how textualized our world has become, that episode should do it. A lot of things depend on the definition of *is*, as both Jacques Derrida and the "Leader of the Free World" have noted. Even those working in a popular medium like commercial film now regularly take up the question of textual reality. Both *The Truman Show* and *Pleasantville*, for example, are about attempts to break out of thoroughly textualized lives. But break out into what — and where? Thinking with Baudrillard, we may wish to ask just what is supposed to lie beyond that tear in the fabric of the artificial world that signifies the end of *The Truman Show*? Is "the real" lurking beyond the backdrop — out there?

Baudrillard leads us to wonder whether there may be some way out of the maze of simulacra in which we find ourselves to real life, the real America. What *is* the real America? Where may we find it? I believe I can answer those questions — but when we find it we may discover that it is actually hyperreal. That is, for us, now, the real may always be elsewhere. Consider, for example, the possibility that the "real" America is the one given textual form by Norman Rockwell, whose work is now being collected and exhibited by adventurous curators of art museums. In Rockwell's images, nostalgia assumes its full meaning — with a vengeance. As Baudrillard suspected, the nostalgic has become the real. In Vladimir Nabokov's novel *Pnin*, the brilliant art teacher, Lake, insists that Norman Rockwell and Salvador Dalí were twins, one of whom had been stolen at birth by gypsies. At the time, this was taken as a funny slur on Dalí, whose work is extremely realistic in its technique, though surreal in content. But now, thanks to Baudrillard and others, it may be possible to see Rockwell as the true surrealist, or rather, a hyperrealist, who broke through the crust of American life into the hyperreal depths of nostalgia that lie below that surface. I wait for the clever curator who has the guts to bring these twins together for a show called "The Surreal and the Hyperreal: Dalí and Rockwell." It will happen, I assure you. Even as I write, a Rockwell exhibit is headed for the Guggenheim in New York. Putting him together with Dalí is only a matter of time.

The *New York Times*, in November 1999, included a piece praising Rockwell and featuring Rockwell's famous *Triple Self-Portrait*, in which he painted himself from the back, sitting in front of his easel. On the easel there is a partially finished portrait of Norman Rockwell. The painter himself is shown, leaning around his painting to gaze at his image in a large mirror (fig. 1). From this image we must also, of course, infer that there is another Norman Rockwell, facing another easel, painting himself from the rear, and, behind that, perhaps, still another, and so on. And where is the real Norman Rockwell in this vertiginous abyss of images? Is he the painter whose back we see; is he the unfinished sketch; is he the frontal image in the represented mirror; or is he the unseen manipulator of these images? Whatever we conclude, we must be troubled by the distance between the position of the painter as represented and the position he had to be in to represent himself in this way.

But there is more to it than that. Let us look more closely at the image. One of the first things we should note is that these different versions do not agree with one another. The pipe in the mirror and the one dangling

1. Norman Rockwell, *Triple Self-Portrait.*

from the jaw of the painter hang downward. The one on the easel points jauntily out and slightly upward. The mirror image and the painter himself wear glasses, and light flashing off them obscures the painter's eyes in the mirror image. But the easel image has prominent eyes and no glasses at all. It looks suspiciously as if the painted painter is painting a flattering image of himself, which the real painter is exposing as false. So where is the reality in this? The reality, I should like to suggest, is in the scene of language called self-portraiture. How can a self-portrait be made except by looking into a mirror or at a photograph? The one thing a painter can never actually see is his or her own face. Always, there must be some sort of mediating element between the painter and that face. A realistic self-portrait is a representation of a representation. Among other things, painting a mirrored face will reverse the left and right of an actual face. Rockwell parted his hair on the left (as we can see looking at the painter's head from the rear), but the mirror image and the sketched face on the easel part theirs on the right. I believe Rockwell wants us to think about the way that even a faithful rendering of what is in the mirror will falsify what the mirror is reflecting.

He also wants us to think about those discrepancies between the image on the easel and the image in the mirror. Portraiture, he seems to be saying, encourages modification of what is there, whether for simple flattery or for some other interpretive purpose, and self-portraiture is even more fraught with possibilities for deception and detachment from the actual, for it is already mediated by the mirror, with, in this case, its distracting frame and golden eagle. Most self-portraits, including those of Rembrandt and van Gogh, do not include the frame of the mirror in which the painter is regarding himself. That is, as in any Hollywood film, the mechanics of the medium are deliberately concealed in most "portraits of the artist." By exposing them, Rockwell is creating a meta-painting, a very postmodernist move for a painter to make — which is, of course, just what we do not expect a Norman Rockwell to do.

There is something funny going on here, which is also detectable in the accoutrements visible in the painting. Tacked to the paper on the easel are some reproductions of other paintings, including two famous self-portraits by Rembrandt and van Gogh. And there is a golden helmet sitting on top of the post holding the easel — another reminder, perhaps, of Rembrandt. Why are these in the painting? Because they were there, you might say, but that simply will not stand up to investigation of the image. If we look closely, we can see that the wastebasket is about to catch fire, that the painter's drink is likely to slip off the book it is resting on, and that the painted image looks younger than the painter in the mirror (who is also painted, of course). One must assume an authorial intention behind these matters. Rockwell put paintings by Rembrandt, van Gogh, Dürer, and Picasso there because he wanted to show us that he could copy them and because he wanted us to be aware of them. Is he comparing himself to these artists? Well, yes he is, I should say, but how seriously? Very seriously, would be my answer, but in a playful manner. Rockwell is an extremely skilled technician of painting who has never been taken seriously because his images are dominated by nostalgia and because they are so frequently narrative or anecdotal. In this painting, as in most of his work, he is telling or suggesting a story, in which events before and after the represented moment are implicated. He commits, regularly, all the sins that high modernist critics like Clement Greenberg and Roger Fry condemned in the narrative painting of the nineteenth century. Even his self-portrait tells a story about his painting himself rather than offering an image of himself. His work is just about as far from pure painting or abstract expressionism as it can be. In this self-portrait, however, he is making the case for himself as an artist — and that case is definitely and specifically recognizable as postmodern. Lest you think I am taking simple Norman further than he would go, I must mention that there is a further development of this painting in a photograph taken by a frequent collaborator of his, in which a fourth image of Rockwell appears, looking on genially from the left of the frame. In this photograph we are given a representation of a representation of the act of representation. The smile on Rockwell's face, however, assures us that he is a maker, not a victim, of this joke. This photograph, then, was, in some sense, anticipated from the beginning. Rockwell has always been fully aware of the potential abyss of representations behind his images.

Should we accept the case I have made for Rockwell as a postmodern artist? We might, I believe, have a very interesting discussion about that issue, but it would draw us even farther away from our immediate concern, which is just how our classrooms should change in order to deal with this textual world, this world of the hyperreal, in which we and our students live. I think Norman Rockwell, who was quite aware he lived in such a world, may have a good deal to offer us if we can use his work properly, and I shall return to that work before concluding, but first I want to step back and look at the problem in a somewhat broader perspective. A little while ago we considered briefly Samuel Johnson's remarks on the topos of nostalgia that dominates the discourse of graybeards, and Roland Barthes's discussion of the scenes of language that shape the discourse of lovers. Let us return to those texts now to consider their possibilities and implications for the craft of reading.

In the epigraph to this essay Gilles Deleuze suggested that doctors and carpenters have a predestined affinity for the signs of wood or of disease. Without considering how seriously he made such a suggestion, I want to use it to position my rather different approach. Yes, we may indeed have gifts that predispose us to certain pursuits, make certain kinds of signs more easily readable for us than others. Nevertheless, I want to insist that the ability to read signs well can be learned — that there is a craft of reading that can be taught and studied. To illustrate this I shall try to plot out a course in textual reality that begins by reading Johnson's *Rambler* No. 50, from which I quoted his remarks on the way the old habitually speak of the young. In this essay Johnson begins by noting that "there are certain fixed and stated reproaches that one part of mankind has in all ages thrown upon another" (Johnson 164), and he concludes by saying that any reader who wishes to live with "honour and decency, must, when he is young, consider that he shall one day be old; and remember, when he is old, that he has once been young" (Johnson 167). These two statements serve to frame the more specific and parodic rendering of the habitual grumbles of the old about the young. Taken together, they also offer a powerful opening for the sort of course in the craft of reading that I am proposing. The first statement insists on the textual nature of human experience, in which the same "fixed and stated reproaches" are continually recycled across the ages. And the final statement suggests a way out of these cycles, available to those who can imagine a future and a past in which they are present, which means imagining just how their thoughts and actions will be constituted by the cultural texts in which they are enmeshed. It is only by taking the power of cultural texts seriously that we may resist, to some extent, that very power.

In the crafty course I am describing, Johnson's essay could provide not only food for thought but also the occasion for compositions in which students attempt to imagine themselves as old (either in the present or their own future) and write from that perspective. Johnson's text could also be the point of departure for consideration of other situations in which we regularly encounter "fixed and stated" utterances — the speeches of politicians, for example, or athletic coaches, of lawyers, or teachers, or even students. The assumption that we do indeed exist in a textual reality — which is just another name for the hyperreal — should enable students to explore all sorts of aspects of that reality. And here is where Roland Barthes's notion of "scenes of language" can expand the possibilities of discussion and composition. For some years, teachers working with a textbook called *Text Book,* in which I had a hand, have used excerpts from Barthes's *Fragments of a Lover's Discourse* as the basis for writing assignments. One of the most successful of these is called "Fragments of a Student's Discourse."

This assignment assumes that students have discussed and come to an understanding of what Barthes means by "scenes of language," and especially the aspects of erotic relationship he discusses in that book (or the excerpts from it in *Text Book*). They are then asked to consider their lives as students in the same way. Are there features of this life that virtually all students find themselves experiencing? Such topics as "the excuse," "being singled out in class," "the crush," places like "the desk," scenes like "the library at midnight," organs like "the brain," and so on begin to emerge as soon as one starts thinking about the life of a student as a collection of "scenes of language." For students this is an opportunity to see their lives differently, and, by giving expression to those scenes, to know them better and endure them more readily. Barthes, of course, seems to delight in the anguish that constitutes a lover's discourse as he sees it, which is pretty much the way that Proust saw it in a text like "Un Amour de Swann." But a clever and ambitious student might even compose a different version of "a lover's discourse," or go on imaginatively to such things as "a father's discourse," "a mother's discourse," "a coach's discourse," "a teacher's discourse" — though I would advise beginning with those bits of textual reality that they know from the inside, like the academic discourse of schools.

Starting with Johnson and Barthes, there are many ways to go in a course exploring textual reality. For many reasons, I do not intend to fill in all those ways on this occasion. Every good, imaginative teacher will think of useful and appropriate texts, I am sure. But I do think there is a role here for films like those I have already mentioned, *The Truman Show* and *Pleasantville*. And in connection with such films, there is certainly a use for Baudrillard's *Simulations*, a very short book that is surprisingly accessible, which could be studied and discussed at some length, offering the basis for a number of writing assignments. In studying Baudrillard, I would emphasize concepts like "nostalgia" and the "hyperreal," and I would encourage students to find and bring to class examples of these processes at work. And here is where I would certainly wish to turn to the work of Norman Rockwell, whom I see as the very prince of hyperreality. To understand Rockwell, I would argue, is to understand America, because he presents our reality the way we want it to be — or, as is so often the case, the way we want it to have been.

I would use Norman Rockwell's visual art in a course on textual reality for many reasons, but one of them would be the way his works turn unerringly to the "scenes of language" that make up the discourse — or textual reality — that is America. Consider figure 2, for example.

This image has appeared with a number of titles. One of them is *The Discovery*. Another is *The Truth About Santa Claus*. In it we see a child who has opened the bottom drawer of a dresser and found in it a Santa Claus costume in mothballs. The child, dressed in pajamas, has turned around to face someone — let us assume a parent — and his face registers an exaggerated, comic dismay. On the top of the dresser there is a pipe, signifying that this is his father's dresser — and also, perhaps, the presence of the pipe-smoking artist himself. This is a scene of language indeed, an early disillusionment, perhaps the first hint for children that the "real" world of their parents is, in fact, hyperreal. From here on, if we remember this experience, we are not sure just what to believe when our parents, teachers, and leaders speak to us. There is a blank mirror above the dresser, and, to the right, a door is open, revealing room after room, like certain Dutch interiors, with a window at the end. Can these images be accidental, simply there when the artist photographed the scene and dumbly sketched in when he converted it to paint? If this were a work by Rockwell's great predecessor in genre painting, Jean Siméon Chardin, we would be alert to look for allegory within the image. I suggest that Rockwell's work will reward a similar kind of attention.

2. Norman Rockwell, *The Truth About Santa Claus;* also called
The Discovery and *The Bottom Drawer.*

The comic excess of the child's expression suggests
further that this scene, and other disillusions that will inevitably follow, are best understood as cultural jokes,
scenes of language that are too common to be tragic, better laughed over than treated with lugubrious pathos.
But those rooms on the right leading to the window offer
a somber corrective to the light-hearted image of the dis-
illusioned child. I have spoken on the phone with Scotty

Ingram, who posed for this picture in 1956. He tells me that the staircase and the rooms leading away from it were not there at all. "They came from Norman's imagination," Scotty said. Indeed they did, and they were meant as an invitation to ours. There are figurines of this image, however, in which those invitations to reflection (mirror) and contemplation (rooms, window) are missing, and even cropped prints in which the mirror is visible but the rooms and the window are not. One has only to look at these reductive versions to see how they diminish the original — and to begin brooding on the way our culture is capable of more thoroughly commodifying even the work of an artist thought by many critics to be nothing but a commodity in the first place.

We must be grateful for these debased images, however, because we can learn from them. By craftily reading what is absent there, we can see more deeply into the image upon which they are based. All texts have their uses for the crafty reader. And, of course, there are the grounds for a writing assignment here. Actually, there is material here for a number of such assignments. The teacher need only pose these questions or others like them: (1) What story does this image tell? (2) Can you recall an episode in your life similar to the one depicted here? and (3) What can you say about the differences between the figurine or cropped image and the picture it is based on? These are obviously questions that assume different levels of sophistication and preparation in those who may answer them, but I offer them to indicate that Rockwell's work will indeed support various levels of inquiry. Let us look further into the pedagogical possibilities of this work.

Figure 3 is called *After the Prom*. It appeared in 1957, but the scene depicted reaches farther back into the past,

3. Norman Rockwell, *After the Prom.*

or rather into Rockwell's nostalgic American hyperreality. Once again, this is a scene of language, a fragment of a student's discourse, set in one of Rockwell's favorite imaginary places, a soda fountain. I remember vividly my own high school prom, which took place eleven years before Rockwell's image appeared. By a weird chain of circumstances, I had a date with a girl I was in love with at the time, though she professes to this day, quite truthfully, I am sure, never to have known it. Anyway, we didn't go to a soda fountain after the prom. We went to a nightclub, where a chain of disasters began that we need not go into at the moment. My point is simply that Rockwell's image is anachronistic, or achronistic — pointing perhaps to Rockwell time and not to any real American moment — and also that everyone who has been to high school knows that the scene of language called Prom Night actually exists. Young students now may need a footnote on the Soda Fountain, but they will get the idea quickly enough and be in a position to read this visual text and compare it to their own experiences. Rockwell doesn't just tell stories. He opens up scenes of language that invite us to tell our own. As you have seen, he almost betrayed me into telling mine.

I ask you to bear with me through one more Rockwell image, after which I shall try to bring this particular scene of language, "the academic essay," to as graceful a conclusion as I can manage. Figure 4 is already well-known in our national iconography.

This is an oil painting, one of four representing *The Four Freedoms,* this one being, of course, freedom of speech. The scene is a town meeting or similar occasion, and the person exercising his right of free speech is a working man, literally in a blue collar, open at his tan and muscular throat. Think Gary Cooper or Jimmy Stewart. Think Frank Capra. There is one woman in the crowd. Her eyes are on the handsome worker. Closer to him are older men in jackets and ties. The expression on the one closest to him is at the heart of the image. How do you read the expression on his face? I see a kind of surprised, grudging admiration, though I do not see agreement. It is a question worth discussing, especially if one is required to justify a reading by specific signs in the represented physiognomy. But what is most easily seen here is the

4. Norman Rockwell, *Freedom of Speech.*

middle-class man of business with his mouth shut, listening to a worker speak his mind on some public issue, represented by the papers visible in various places, including the worker's pocket. If we look closely, we can see that these papers are the financial report of some town in Vermont. The man is literate and eloquent, and Main Street is giving him a hearing. What kind of reality is this? That is the great question emerging from such a text, an image that gives textual reality to an American dream which is definitely in trouble at the turn of the millennium. Is it a historical reality, a reality of our past, or was it always just a dream, a scene of language that was never actually enacted?

An early version of this image exists, in which Rockwell was still trying to find the right elements for his concept and arrange them in the most effective way. It positions the viewer farther away from the central figure and does not look up at him from the audience, as the final work does. In this sketch all the parts are there but neither defined nor arranged with anything like the power of the final image. Rockwell, of course, was never just a painter but a painter of a special kind: an iconographer, a creator of ideologically charged images. Much of his crafty power in this mode of representation can be understood by comparing a draft like this one to the finished work. For students learning the craft of reading, this sort of project is ideal. And such projects are already being undertaken in classrooms all over this country. The traveling show "Norman Rockwell: Pictures for the American People," which is on its way to the Guggenheim, offers on the World Wide Web a well-conceived "Resource Packet for Educators," with suggestions for discussion of Rockwell's images at various grade levels. Here are some of the suggestions in the packet for teaching *Triple Self-Portrait:*

Background

Norman Rockwell's *Triple Self-Portrait* is full of details that give insight into his life. For example: the metal bucket with a bit of smoke rising from within probably refers to Norman Rockwell's Vermont studio fire in 1943. Describing this fire with sketches in his autobiography, Rockwell said, "In a way the fire was a good thing. It cleaned out the cobwebs." The glass of Coca-Cola is present because Rockwell enjoyed this soft drink. The helmet refers to an incident that happened to him during a trip to Paris. These props were specially chosen for this picture. They are not there by accident, but by design. Other interesting facts on this picture are:

- Norman Rockwell's *Triple Self-Portrait* appeared on the cover of the February 13, 1960, *Saturday Evening Post*. This issue began a weekly series of articles drawn from his autobiography, *My Adventures as an Illustrator*.

- Throughout art history, artists have explored the idea of the self-portrait. Norman Rockwell admired the work of other artists, among them Dürer, Rembrandt, Picasso, and Van Gogh. Their self-portraits are tacked to Rockwell's canvas for inspiration.

- While Rockwell did many self-portraits over the years, it's this one, done when the artist was 66 years old, that is the most famous and has been most often parodied.

- Compare the Norman Rockwell you see in the mirror with the version on the canvas. Why do you think he would paint different versions of himself?

- The tools of painting scattered on the floor play an important role in the composition of the painting. This picture has a white background and needs the paint brushes and tubes of paint to create the illusion of a floor. Without these items, everything else in the picture would appear to be floating in space.

- Diagonal lines created by the paintbrushes bring you into the picture and lead your eye to the stool, then to Norman Rockwell and finally to the various versions of himself he has painted. (Rockwell Packet 14)

These suggestions are oriented to a course in art for very young students, but they point toward the sort of discussion that I have been proposing. I have been using Rockwell's images to suggest ways of organizing a course in textual reality that would raise questions about the real and the hyperreal, about the way ideology shapes perception and representation, about the scenes of language that organize our lives. Such a course would aim at changing its students in many ways, ranging from improvement in essential verbal skills to a sharper sense of the mediated nature of their world and their lives — our world and our lives. There may well be other and better ways to do this, but I am certain that this way will work. To understand the craft of reading is to understand the world itself as a text and to be able to read it critically. The crafty reader will not mistake signs of the hyperreal for instances of reality. Warned by such examples as Rockwell's deconstruction of his own self-portrait, such a reader will be attuned to the power of images like those of Norman Rockwell to shape our thoughts and feelings about life itself.

Heavy Reading

The Monstrous Personal Chronicle as a Genre

It is a narrative of daily life, mean happenings, little people. Here are no lessons for the world, no disclosures to
shock people. It is filled with trivial things, partly that no
one mistake for history the bones from which some day a
man may make history, and partly for the pleasure it gave
me to recall.

I am a camera with its shutter open, quite passive, recording, not thinking. . . . Some day this will all have to be developed, carefully printed, fixed.

This experience made me say to myself, "If a Roman
woman had, some years before the sack of Rome, realized
why it was going to be sacked and what motives inspired
the barbarians and what the Romans, and had written
down all she knew and felt about it, the record would have
been of value to historians. My situation, though probably
not so fatal, is as interesting." Without doubt it was my
duty to keep a record of it.

Reading Gide's diaries. . . . An interesting knotted book.
It's queer that diaries now pullulate. No one can settle to a
work of art. Comment only. . . . It's the comment, the daily
interjection, that comes handy in times like these. I too feel it.

My four epigraphs are taken from works written by English men and women between the late 1920s and 1941. As a group, they should help us identify and begin to think about a literary phenomenon of the period, which is the flourishing, or, as one of the four remarked astringently, the pullulating, of diaries, journals, reflections, and other forms of prose composition marked by very personal perspectives, on the one hand, and a certain looseness of form, on the other. The first of these four quotations comes from T. E. Lawrence's narrative of his experiences during the First World War, *Seven Pillars of Wisdom*. For our purposes what is important here is the emphasis on the quotidian, the little personal events that are emphatically *not* history, that are both too small and too raw, too inchoate, to constitute a grand historical narrative. Here are bones, says Lawrence, who was trained as an archaeologist, that are not yet articulated by the historian's conceptual apparatus.

The second quotation, probably the most recognizable of the four, comes from the opening page of Christopher Isherwood's *Goodbye to Berlin*, which was made into a play called *I Am a Camera* and then reached a vast audience as the musical drama and film *Cabaret*. Isherwood's passivity in the Berlin of the thirties is extremely different from the active engagement of Lawrence of Arabia in World War I, yet his text echoes Lawrence's in its insistence on its raw, formless quality. The significant difference, of course, lies in Isherwood's metaphor from cinematography. A still camera with its shutter open will record nothing—or a blur, but a movie camera will indeed record what passes in front of it. But this is a negative only, not developed, not fixed. Both Lawrence and

Isherwood insist on the unfinished quality of their texts, but they also strongly imply that this very lack of final articulation gets them close to reality — closer than a fully conceptualized work of history or an edited cinematic text ever could. By using the film developer's term *fixed*, Isherwood suggests that actuality resists such articulation, even as Lawrence's bones may be realer than any history constructed from them. We need not, at the moment, worry about the justice of such claims. We need only note that they are similar in their preference for the inarticulate, even though one records adventures in the First World War while the other documents a passive response to the approach of the Second.

My third epigraphic excerpt comes from Rebecca West's extraordinary book on Yugoslavia just before World War II, *Black Lamb and Grey Falcon*. I quote it here mainly to indicate how close it is conceptually to Lawrence's formulation. Something is being written that is not history but comes before history, something that will interest historians because it is a document. Of course West's Roman woman is already on the way to historicizing, since she knows the "motivations" of history's actors, but my point is that West wants to distance what she is doing from what historians do. Like Lawrence and Isherwood, she wants the authority not of the generalizing historian but of the personal observer, whose feelings about events are as important as her knowledge. This is different from Isherwood's claim, because a camera does not feel, but it is similar in its insistence on an immediate relation to a certain reality, which she is documenting. West's stress on gender — a Roman woman, not a man — seems to go with her insistence that feelings are important. This is an issue to which we shall return later on.

The fourth quotation comes from Virginia Woolf's diary for 1939. She does not bother, in this instance, to justify the diary as a document. It is not her primary form of writing. At that time, in fact, she was working on both her biography of Roger Fry and the novel that became *Between the Acts* and had just published *Three Guineas*. I have quoted her here, however, because she is aware of the phenomenon I shall be discussing and offers the beginning of an explanation for it. As she sees it, diaries "pullulate" because writers cannot settle to their art with the war on yet must continue to write, for writing is a comfort. It "comes in handy." She is right about this, I am sure, yet diaries had been pullulating for more than a decade when she wrote these words. It was not only the war, then, but something about the whole period between the two world wars that led so many writers to work in the mode that I am calling the monstrous personal chronicle. This, too, is a topic to which we shall return.

What I mean by that cumbersome term "monstrous personal chronicle" will take some explaining. In explaining it, I shall also take up the theme of the usefulness of generic notions in the craft of reading. For here we have a real test case. I shall be arguing that by inventing a new generic notion, we can in fact read certain texts with greater comprehension and appreciation, and also that these new filiations will help us to understand more adequately the culture of the period between World Wars I and II as it was experienced by men and women who wrote in English and lived in Britain or on the European continent. This will not be the place, however, to discuss definitively the nature and usefulness of generic concepts for the craft of reading. I shall postpone that until the next essay, in which the theory of genres will loom large. Here I must simply get about the business of defining this one, which will be a somewhat heavy and complicated affair.

To speak of a kind of writing called the monstrous personal chronicle, we must begin with some definitions:

> *Chronicle.* A narrative organized by time rather than by a plot. Chronicle is often thought of as a form of temporal document that preceded the writing of what is properly called history, as in the chronicles of monasteries and convents. It is just a record, not a story, nor yet an explanation. In a sense, chronicle is the most primitive form of narrative.

> *Personal chronicle.* The narrative in question belongs to the writer. The writer's life and times are being described. Diaries, journals, and memoirs are personal chronicles. Autobiographies, on the other hand, often have more of a plot, especially those that lead toward a moment of vocation or achievement, in which the writer's character is defined or some particular goal is reached. They are not, then, chronicles, in the sense of that term as it is used here. All this is clear enough. The crucial question for our purposes, however, is what makes a personal chronicle "monstrous."

> *Monstrosity.* Sheer size, to be sure, can constitute monstrosity, but I would argue that this is inherent in the form itself. Even early diaries,

like those of Pepys and Evelyn, run to considerable length. If a writer records his or her life regularly and lives a long time, a very large personal chronicle will be the result. But size alone is not enough — nor is it absolutely required — to constitute monstrosity as I am defining it here. From its earliest uses in English, the word has connoted something misshapen, unnatural. Among the examples offered by the OED are references to a child with three hands (1300) and to a woman using weapons (1558), suggesting that the word covered everything from what was physically "unnatural" to what was considered socially inappropriate.

Monstrous personal chronicle. We can begin by thinking of this quasi-genre in terms of monstrosity of form and monstrosity of content before we examine the complex interaction of the two. Monstrosity of form at its simplest is merely lack of shape, a lack of formal necessity in the ordering and relation of the parts of the text, coupled with an excess of size. But there is a more complex formal monstrosity that comes from an uneasy fusion of the processes of fiction with those of the document. We can find a simple example of this in Christopher Isherwood's *Berlin Stories,* where the narrator of the first of the two volumes included in this text is called William Bradshaw, while the narrator in the second volume is called Christopher Isherwood, though both live in exactly the same place at the same time. But the interaction of fictional and documentary impulses in the monstrous personal chronicle are rich and complex, constituting a major element of the genre's formal monstrosity. Monstrosity of content in these texts ranges from attention to matters hitherto considered unpublishable, as in the obsessive sexuality of Henry Miller's *Tropic of Cancer*, to the monstrosity of history itself, in a period after one horrible war and before one that many people felt was bound to come and bring worse horrors. The dissolution of the old empires also made itself felt in European writing during this period, along with the threat of newer totalitarian regimes like the Thousand-Year Reich promised by Hitler. And both these historical processes (that is, the dismantling of the Ottoman Empire, the Hapsburg Empire, and even the British Empire, as well as the threatened rise of new Nazi and Fascist empires) seemed to require a monstrous documentary form to represent them.

My notion of formal monstrosity can be illustrated by examining a fascinating moment in the second volume of Siegfried Sassoon's autobiography, *The Weald of Youth*, when he must face the fact that he has already presented much of this material in a sequence of autobiographical novels:

> In this "real autobiography" of mine I have hitherto done what I could to avoid the

subject of fox-hunting, for the excellent reason that it has already been monopolized by a young man named George Sherston [in Sassoon's *Memoirs of a Fox-Hunting Man*]. To tell the truth, I am a little shy of trespassing on Sherston's territory. I should not like to feel that I had in any way impaired his reality in the minds of his appreciative friends, for many of whom he is, perhaps, more alive than the present writer. And to assert that he was "only me with a lot left out" sounds off-hand and uncivil. (Sassoon 66)

Among the fascinations of this passage are the layers of truth and reality evoked by it. It is in some sense the reality, the "alive" quality of the fictional character that seems to efface the presence of his creator, now that he is attempting to put in some of what got "left out" in Sherston's fictional memoir — which was obviously not very fictional to begin with. Sassoon plays with this problem for a couple of pages and declares it resolved or, at any rate, "ushered out," but what remains for our consideration is his description of what has happened — which, he says, "was a collision between fictionalized reality and essayized autobiography" (68–69).

This collision resulted from Sassoon's somewhat strange decision to go over the same periods of his life in two different modes, but the generic problem is actually even more complicated than his description would have us believe. In reality, both texts have a good deal left out. Both are written in the form of an autobiographical memoir, one by the fictional Sherston and the other by Sassoon, in much the same prose style. They are both autobiographical, both fictional, and both "essayized." But one, the one in which the author writes as himself, claims not to contradict the other but to fill in some gaps it has left, to tell a somewhat different story: the "truth" about how the writer came to be the poet Siegfried Sassoon, whose works are known and respected. The fiction, in this view, was designed more to please the reader, the autobiography more to inform that same reader, but both books read alike, both are charming, digressive, and evocative of the Weald, that lovely wooded part of Kent and Sussex.

I do not wish to lean too heavily on the epistemological problems raised by Sassoon's texts but simply to notice that the two together force us to be aware of such problems and the generic difficulties that go with them. It is the fact of their coexistence in the same biographical space that affects us in a particularly modern way, forcing us to be aware of the literariness of both texts, and of the complex relationship between the personal chronicle as life and as art. Either set of texts standing alone would be far less troubling — the personal novel or the novelistic autobiography — but their combination is monstrous, though in a gentle, civilized way. Thinking along these lines, one will detect other forms of monstrosity in these texts.

His vantage point is so firmly anchored in the world Sassoon inhabited after his devastating experience in the Great War that he often thinks of himself as a ghost visiting this vanished world of his youth, unseen by his earlier self and the others who inhabit it. He returns to it twice — as the "fictional" Sherston and as the "real" Siegfried, a doppelgänger indeed — because he is obsessed by it, by its beauty and by its lostness. The difference between the two texts, slight as it is, is his excuse for his ghostly returns to that enchanted past, a past that is enchanted because the Great War itself has intervened to change the present utterly from that earlier way of life. "The past," as L. P. Hartley said so memorably in the first sentence of *The Go-Between*, "is a foreign country; they do things differently there." The present tense, as used by Hartley here, emphasizes the living quality of that past, while the spatial metaphor (a foreign country) stresses its alien nature, its incomprehensible distance from the present. Out of such feelings, one kind of monstrosity is born. But there are others, as we shall see in the discussion to come.

Virginia Woolf hinted at something out of control when she described personal chronicles as "pullulating," with its connotations of teeming or swarming. She was thinking, of course, not of the internal dynamic of certain texts but of the way that personal chronicles were appearing in great numbers, apparently overwhelming more deliberately artistic texts at the end of the 1930s. It will be useful for us, however, to consider the way that these large and shapeless and personal monsters were a reaction against the modernist imperative to be objective (as in Eliot's "objective correlative"), to efface personality, and, above all, to produce (in that key phrase of Bloomsbury aesthetics) "significant form." In response to modernism's cultural imperatives — especially the privileging of the artistic genius — the monstrous personal chronicle allows an author to establish credentials as a genius or artist while evading any responsibility for the creation of an aesthetic masterpiece.

The thirties were haunted by the imperative that Cyril Connolly expressed so powerfully in the opening sentence of *The Unquiet Grave* (1945): "The more books we read, the sooner we perceive that the true function of a writer is to produce a masterpiece, and that no other task is of any consequence" (Connolly 1). Yet the writers of the age were also driven by other imperatives that led in other directions. One such imperative was to make their own lives into works of art, as Oscar Wilde, among others, had urged, which led to the impasse described succinctly by W. B. Yeats: perfection of the life or of the work, but not both. Another was to bear witness to their times, which they felt might be obliterated without an adequate record. This led to yet another impasse, for to bear witness adequately was to give up all pretensions to art, as Jean-Paul Sartre explained so powerfully in the forties in *What Is Literature?* Feeling, as anyone might, the impossibility of responding adequately to these imperatives, certain writers seized upon the monstrous fictionalized chronicle of an artist-writer's daily life as a solution — producing not masterpieces but texts that would nevertheless demand serious attention. If their lives were insufficiently artistic, they would improve them in the telling. If the work lacked shape and structure, it would compel by its monstrosity or its scandalous revelations. And it would record, lovingly, details too trivial or obscene for what had been called literature. They would be resolutely modern, then, but not exactly in the way Joyce, Pound, or Eliot were modern (though there is more than a touch of this impulse in *Ulysses* and *The Cantos*) — closer, perhaps, to the modern ways of Proust and D. H. Lawrence. Above all, they would assert their modernity by chronicling their own, new experiences. And if necessary, they would go to extremes to have experiences that were indubitably new. Which meant, in many cases, that they were driven to outlandish actions in order to have experiences worthy of chronicling.

These texts that I am attempting to describe tend to be large. That is a frequent though not crucial aspect of their "monstrosity." I am thinking of works like Dorothy Richardson's *Pilgrimage,* the lightly fictionalized chronicle of her life in thirteen volumes, begun in 1915 and terminated (not finished) with her death in 1957; of Virginia Woolf's *Diary,* begun in 1915, ending just four days before her death in 1941; and especially of Anaïs Nin's journals or diaries, begun in 1914 and continued through sixty-nine notebook-volumes into the early forties (and in folders until her death in the seventies — but the thirties volumes are what I shall be focusing on here). During this same period some of the best writers in English also produced large chronicles dealing with encounters with Others — works for which the generic designation "travelogue" seems woefully inadequate, though they are not exactly journals or diaries either.

T. E. Lawrence's *Seven Pillars of Wisdom,* which recounts his adventures in Arabia during World War I, appeared first, in 1926. George Orwell chronicled his sustained attempt to transcend his class position ("lower-upper-middle class," he called it) in *Down and Out in Paris and London* (1933), *The Road to Wigan Pier* (1937), and *Homage to Catalonia* (1938), works that tower over his novels of the same period. Vera Brittain's *Testament of Youth* appeared in 1933 and is read and discussed today, though her novels are forgotten. Stevie Smith's three-volume sequence of autobiographical fiction, beginning with *Novel on Yellow Paper* (1936), is still underappreciated, partly because it has not been seen through the right generic spectacles. Rebecca West's major work has turned out to be *Black Lamb and Grey Falcon,* her account of the present and past of Yugoslavia, written in the late thirties, published in 1942, reissued in 1982, and still in print despite running to nearly 1,200 fine-printed pages in length. Though West's book is absolutely crammed with the history and descriptions of Yugoslavian people and places, it has been called by John Gunther (who made T. E. Lawrence into a media icon) "not so much a book about Yugoslavia as a book about Rebecca West" (quoted in Glendinning 164). It is, in fact both, but in a fashion that challenged conventional notions of objectivity. The central episode in T. E. Lawrence's massive chronicle of the war in Arabia, the account of his capture and sexual abuse by Turkish soldiers, may be an invention, and whatever its foundation in reality, it was certainly fictionalized in the course of its many manuscript revisions. *Seven Pillars,* too, is a book more about Lawrence than about Arabia. Yet both Lawrence and West were not only writing about themselves, they were writing about nationalist ferment in the wake of the dead Ottoman Empire and the dying Hapsburg Empire, and against the machinations of European powers grimly hanging on to their imperial ambitions.

The suggestion I am making is that during the period that extends from just before the First World War to just after the Second, much of the best writing that appeared in English prose took the form of extended chronicles in which the personal was neither suppressed nor transcended in the approved modernist manner, but was kept in the foreground, sometimes flaunted, but always acknowledged, and that this attention to the personal compensates for the modernist attention to form and structure that is so obviously lacking. This was also a genre in which women worked very well. I am not prepared to argue that this is a species of *écriture féminine*, though some of these writers — especially Richardson, Nin, and Woolf — made exactly that argument, with conviction and persuasive power. When Nin read some praise of Richardson in 1931, she reacted strongly: "Had a terrible fright, thinking someone had usurped my place, or rather, preceded me in literature. But it was a false alarm. Not me, not me, but it is very good" (quoted in Bair 545, n.5).

It may be worth noting in passing that Virginia Woolf also worried about her relation to Richardson. When she reviewed *The Tunnel* in *TLS* in 1919, she observed that "the reader is not provided with a story; he is invited to embed himself in Miriam Henderson's consciousness" (Woolf 1: 257–58, n. 32). And she declined to review the next volume, *Interim*, recording in her own diary that "when I looked at it, I found myself looking for faults; hoping for them. And they would have bent my pen, I know. There must be an instinct of self-preservation at work. If she's good then I'm not" (Woolf 1: 315). Woolf's objectivity, plainly in evidence here, is a vast distance from the subjectivity that is at the heart of the genre I am trying to describe. Yet her diaries are immensely readable now precisely because her personality dominates and animates them so powerfully. As a diarist she is very different from that Princess of Liars, Anaïs Nin. Nevertheless, the anxiety that is ever present in these diaries — anxiety about the reception of her work, anxiety about retaining her sanity, and, finally, anxiety about war — can be seen as the shadow of a monstrosity that colors even these luminous pages. The personal chronicle, of course, is still very much with us as a literary form. But in the period of the two world wars, public events put private lives under a special pressure that elevated the personal to a level of greater intensity and interest, and it is this pressure of history on personal lives that gives these texts their monstrous intensity.

Vera Brittain can serve as an example of the relation between this form of writing and the historical situation of the writers. Like many others, she did not mean to produce a monstrous personal chronicle when she started trying to write about her experiences as a V.A.D. nurse during and after World War I:

> My original idea was that of a long novel, and I started to plan it. To my dismay it turned out to be a hopeless failure; I never got much further than the planning, for I found that the people and the events about which I was writing were still too near and too real to be made the subjects of an imaginative, detached reconstruction.
>
> Then I tried the effect of reproducing parts of the long diary which I kept from 1913 to 1918, with fictitious names substituted for the real ones out of consideration for the many persons still alive who were mentioned in it with a youthful and sometimes rather cruel candour. This too was a failure. . . .
>
> There was only one possible course left — to tell my own fairly typical story as truthfully as I could. . . . In no other fashion, it seemed, could I carry out my endeavour to put the life of an ordinary individual into its

niche in contemporary history, and thus illustrate the influence of world-wide events and
movements upon the personal destinies of
men and women. (Brittain 11–12)

Two of Brittain's observations here are important for our
purposes. First she tried both the way of fiction and then
the way of pure document. Neither worked, so she found
a middle way, the writing of a personal chronicle. But the
chronicle was not merely personal. It was a deliberate attempt to connect the personal to the historical, which she
found she could accomplish only by working in the form
of a personal chronicle. History provided the monstrosity she chronicled. The war took the lives of her fiancé,
her friends, and finally her beloved brother. It also
forced her to look directly at monstrosity in her role as a
nurse: "Although the first dressing at which I assisted —
a gangrenous leg wound, slimy and green and scarlet,
with the bone laid bare — turned me sick and faint for a
moment that I afterwards remembered with humiliation,
I minded what I described to Roland as 'the general at-
mosphere of inhumanness' far more than the grotesque
mutilations of bodies and limbs and faces" (211).

In order to endure what they must endure and see
what they must see, the nurses needed to repress their
own humanity. Brittain saw this happening around her
and feared that she would lose her own identity in this
service. "After the Somme I had seen men without faces,
without eyes, without limbs, men almost disemboweled,
men with hideous truncated stumps of bodies," she
writes, thinking of a friend who has just received a "serious" wound, wondering just what lies behind that vague,
terrifying word. Even some distance from the front, dur-

ing a stint on Malta, she feels that the wind carries "the sound of great guns bludgeoning the battered remnants of men and trenches into ghoulish anonymity" (337–38). "The world was mad and we were all victims" (376), she concludes. After the war, returning to Somerville College, Oxford, she suffered from nightmares and hallucinations, seeing her own face in the mirror as bearded like a witch, and hearing herself (and the other young women there) described by a "senile placid don" in Virgilian language, as a "*monstrum horrendum informe*" (508), a "horrible shapeless monster." How else to respond to this, represent this life and this world, but by means of a monstrous personal chronicle?

In very different circumstances, but faced with a similar problem, Christopher Isherwood also began by thinking of putting what he had seen into the form of a traditional novel:

> My first idea, immediately after leaving Berlin in 1933, was to transform this material into one huge tightly constructed melodramatic novel, in the manner of Balzac. . . .
>
> Maybe Balzac himself could have devised a plot-structure which would plausibly contain the mob of characters I wanted to introduce to my readers. The task was quite beyond my powers. What I actually produced was an absurd jumble of subplots and coincidences which defeated me whenever I tried to straighten it out on paper. (Isherwood v)

Vera Brittain called the plot of the novel she tried to write about her experiences "lurid" (447), and Isherwood described his as "melodramatic." Both of them, without formulating some modernist set of objections to the realistic novel, simply found that the form wouldn't work for them, given the experiences they wished to represent in their texts. In Brittain's case these experiences were mainly the First World War and the immediate postwar period, while for Isherwood it was the Berlin scene of the early 1930s during Hitler's rise to power, but in both cases it was the clash of certain actualities with a "realistic" tradition that required too much plot, turning those actual events into something "lurid" or "melodramatic." Realism, it seems, wasn't real enough. Which didn't prevent either writer from using the devices of traditional novelistic plotting when it suited them, as when Brittain ends a chapter with these words:

> The next morning I had just finished dressing, and was putting the final touches to the pastel-blue crêpe-de-Chine blouse, when the expected message came to say that I was wanted on the telephone. Believing that I was at last to hear the voice for which I had waited for twenty-four hours, I dashed joyously into the corridor. But the message was not from Roland but from Clare; it was not to say that he had arrived home that morning, but to tell me that he had died of wounds at a Casualty Clearing Station on December 23rd. (236)

Isherwood also used the devices of fiction freely and expertly in composing the *Berlin Stories*. It was not fiction that he and Brittain found wanting but the norms of the traditionally plotted novel, the same norms that the more overtly experimental modernists resisted in other ways. Even though he suppressed almost all traces of the homoerotic impulse that had brought him to Berlin in the first place and held him there for some years (discussed fully in *Christopher and His Kind*), *The Berlin Stories*, like Brittain's *Testament of Youth*, were chronicles of individual lives dominated by powerful historical forces — in this case the rise of Nazism. The real end of the book comes a few lines before the last words, in this sentence: "The sun shines, and Hitler is master of this city" (*GB* 207). The very rationality of the realistic form seemed inappropriate, since, as Brittain put it, "the universe had become irrational" (288). The monstrous personal chronicle offered a solution. But there were a number of ways in which a chronicle could become monstrous. Henry Miller found one that suited him.

Miller's *Tropic of Cancer* comes to us now with praise on the cover assuring us that it is "ONE OF THE GREAT NOVELS OF OUR CENTURY." Great it may be, but it is surely not a novel, as Karl Shapiro, who wrote the introduction to the current Grove Press edition, knew very well. "Every word he has ever written is autobiographical" (vi), says Shapiro shrewdly. He then tries to name the kind of writing we find in Miller's book and finally settles on "personal apocalyptic prose" (xii). Miller himself says that "the book has begun to grow inside me," and adds that "it is colossal in its pretentiousness." Finally, he says, speaking of another project in words that partly suit the book he is actually writing, "It will be enormous, the Book" (26, 27), and he goes into one of his quasi-surrealistic rhapsodies, in which the book takes shape as a cathedral of "murderous insouciance." His method, clearly, is not realistic. His goal, however, is the *real,* which he feels can be reached in language only by way of the surreal. Speaking of the great writers he admires from the past, his "idols," he says, "When I think of their deformities, of the monstrous styles they chose, of the flatulence and tediousness of their works, of all the chaos and confusion they wallowed in, of the obstacles they heaped up around them, I feel an exaltation" (252–53). For Miller, monstrosity of style is the only path to reality. "If a man ever dared to translate all that is in his heart, to put down what is really his experience, what is truly his truth, I think the world would go to smash" (249). But to do this strong words are needed, "words . . . stronger than the lying crushing weight of the world" (248–49).

Clearly, *Tropic of Cancer* is a monstrous personal chronicle itself and an argument for the necessity of a monstrous art as a response to a world that is "used up and polished like a leper's skull" (248) — a response to a culture that Miller saw in terms of "the creaking machinery of humanity" (254). Just as clearly, Miller's monstrosity, and that of his writing, are different from those of Isherwood and Brittain. But these very differences are evidence of how powerfully all these writers felt both the monstrosity of their world and the inadequacy of traditional forms for the representation of that world. There are many modernities, and one of them is to be found in that no-man's land between the quotidian and the surreal. Texts like Miller's and Isherwood's, so close to their lives, have loose structures and vague outlines. These narratives are continued in other books, and even revised, as Isherwood revised his Berlin chronicle by revealing in *Christopher and His Kind* things that he had concealed in the earlier narratives.

If we think of modernism in literature as a practice linked to New Criticism as a way of reading, we can see that these monstrous personal chronicles could never be accepted in a modernist canon based on New Critical principles. My position, I hope, is clear. Too bad for the canon and its principles. These are interesting, important texts, fully worthy of any craft of reading we can bring to bear upon them. But to read them with appreciation and critical intelligence we need to recognize that they require a different set of generic expectations than those we bring to both the traditional novel and the tightly constructed modernist work of fiction. We need to expect a looseness of structure, a lack of final closure in many instances. In these texts we find writing that allows for essayistic excursions, writers who put things in their accounts simply because they happened, volumes in which the intimate aspects of the author's bodily existence are often front and center — whether it is Anaïs Nin enumerating the types of orgasms she experiences or George Orwell explaining exactly what it is like to be hit by a bullet. Something modern but not modernist in the usual sense of that word is happening here.

We can see it happening in the writing of Gertrude Stein, for example, when she undertakes to write *The Autobiography of Alice B. Toklas*. Stein herself situated her textual achievement not in *The Autobiography* but in her earlier *Making of Americans*, which she described in *The Autobiography* as "a monumental work which was the beginning, really the beginning of modern writing" (215). Whether "monumental" in this case equals "monstrous," I leave to other readers, but Stein described it as "a book one thousand pages long, closely printed on large pages" (223), in which "the sentences, as the book goes on, get longer and longer" (224). *The Making of Americans* is indeed a chronicle of sorts, but it is not exactly personal. As she wrote it, Stein tells us through her mask as Toklas, "It had changed from being a history of a family to being a history of everybody the family knew and then it became the history of every kind and of every individual human being" (113). *The Autobiography,* on the other hand, is most certainly a personal chronicle, but is it monstrous? There is surely something a bit monstrous about writing, in the first person, the autobiography of another person, who is alive and quite capable of writing her own. In fact, when Alice did come to write her own autobiography much later (1963), she had to find another name for it, so she called it *What Is Remembered.* Stein's *The Autobiography of Alice B. Toklas* begins with these words: "I was born in San Francisco, California" (3). *What Is Remembered* begins with these: "I was born and raised in California" (3). Writing her own autobiography, poor Alice cannot help but see the enormous footprints of Gertrude all over her path.

The monstrous events recorded by Brittain and others lie behind Stein's personal chronicle as well. She notes, at the end of chapter 5, that "in this spring and early summer of nineteen fourteen the old life was over" (142). And later, "It was a confused world" (189); "It was a restless and disturbed world" (190); "It was a changed Paris. Guillaume Apollinaire was dead" (190). But her prose never loses its placid energy and her truly monstrous but endearing egoism never falters. The book ends with these words: "About six weeks ago Gertrude Stein said, it does not look to me as if you were ever going to write that autobiography. You know what I am going to do. I am going to write it for you. I am going to write it as simply as Defoe did the autobiography of Robinson Crusoe. And she has and this is it" (252). The book ends, not as Proust's monstrous novel does, with the narrator now ready to begin his great work, but with the supposed author being told that someone else was not only going to do it but had already done it. If the cover had not told us that Stein was the author, this is the first we would know of it.

This is a sort of monstrosity, as I have been suggesting, but it is not the end of Stein's chronicle. The story continues, but now with Gertrude assuming the mask of her own voice (Picasso, you remember, said that she would come to resemble the mask he used in place of her "realistic" face in his portrait of her), in a book called, modestly, *Everybody's Autobiography* (1938). This one begins with a preface in which Stein observes, "Alice B. Toklas did hers and now everybody will do theirs" (xxi). The book then continues with a chapter called "What Happened After the Autobiography of Alice B. Toklas" and ends with "now it is today" (278). There was nothing to prevent further volumes from appearing, except Stein's death in 1946. Many of the chronicles we are considering are, in principle, continuable as long as the writer is alive. Even Vera Brittain, who gave *Testament of Youth* a quasi-novelistic conclusion by ending it with her marriage, found it necessary to write other "Testaments" later on. But Stein's writing in her personal chronicles is not so experimental as it is in many of her other works. What is truly monstrous about her oeuvre is that all the works, the "portraits," the essays, the poems, and the chronicles themselves, can and should be read as if (as Shapiro said of Miller) "every word is autobiographical."

Of all the writers in English at this time, however, the one whose work seems to embody the generic potential of the monstrous personal chronicle most fully is undoubtedly Anaïs Nin. Henry Miller was quite aware of this, for he came very close to describing this generic concept in an essay on Nin called "Un Être étoilique," which first appeared in T. S. Eliot's magazine, *The Criterion:*

> The importance of such a work for our time hardly needs to be stressed. More and more, as our era draws to a close, are we made aware of the tremendous significance of the human document. Our literature, unable any longer to express itself through dying forms, has become almost exclusively biographical. The artist is retreating behind the dead forms to rediscover in himself the eternal source of creation. Our age, intensely productive, yet thoroughly unvital, uncreative, is obsessed with a lust for investigating the mysteries of the personality. We turn instinctively to those documents — fragments, notes, autobiographies, diaries — which appease our hunger for life because, avoiding the circuitous expression of art, they seem to put us directly in contact with that which we are seeking. I say "seem to" because there are no short cuts such as we imagine, because the most direct expression, the most permanent and the most effective, is always that of art. The diary is an art form just as much as the novel or the play. The diary simply requires a greater canvas; it is a chronological tapestry. (Miller, *Reader* 288)

Miller's essay in *The Criterion* brought a lot of attention to Nin's unpublished diaries. Even Jean Paulhan of the *Nouvelle Revue Française* considered publishing an excerpt. At that time either he or his coeditor (there are two versions of the story) observed, "We must study this diary, what it really is, for of course in Mr Miller's essay there is a lot about Mr Miller" (quoted in Nin, *Journals*, 2: 273; Bair 242). But Nin's diary proved to be impossible for Paulhan to publish, as it did for an extraordinary number of other editors and publishing houses. They worried about lawsuits from those mentioned, even if the names were disguised, and they worried about prosecution for obscenity. Some, to be sure, simply did not like the work, but most could not see how to shape this monster into a profitable book. As a monster, it could scarcely be published, but, without its monstrosity, it was less interesting and less marketable. It was, as Gertrude Stein told Hemingway about one of his stories, "*inaccrochable*," unhangable, like a painting that could not be displayed in a gallery without enraging the public. Nin's most reliable biographer, Deirdre Bair, observed dryly that when Paulhan was "confronted with the reality of the woman's writing rather than the man's refracted view of it, he decided it was not appropriate for his august publication" (Bair 242).

But what, exactly, was monstrous about Nin's diary? In his *Criterion* essay, Miller had compared it — and Nin — to a whale, a great monster of the deep:

> For in a way this diary of Anaïs Nin is also a curious dream of something or other, a dream which takes place fathoms deep below the surface of the sea. . . . Everyone who comes

under her glance is lured, as it were, into a spider web, stripped bare, dissected, dismembered, devoured and digested. All without malice! Done automatically as part of life's processes. The person who is doing all this is really an innocent little creature tucked away in the lining of the belly of the whale. In nullifying herself she really becomes this great leviathan which swims the deep and devours everything in sight. (303)

Nin's diary is indeed monstrous, both large and essentially shapeless — not confused or disorganized but constantly reorganized and rewritten to the point where a single definitive edition of it is almost impossible, except as a kind of hypertextual mélange of versions. For example, *The Diary of Anaïs Nin,* volume 1, *1931–1934,* covers the same time period as *Henry and June: From the Unexpurgated Diary of Anaïs Nin* (which covers mainly the year 1932), and *Incest: From "A Journal of Love"* (which claims to be *The Unexpurgated Diary of Anaïs Nin, 1932–1934*). The implication is that there is a single "unexpurgated" diary somewhere, from which these versions are excerpts or sections, but it is impossible to put them together into a single sequence at those points where they could be expected to match up.

The central episode of *Incest* is Nin's affair with her father in June of 1932. The erotic exploits lovingly detailed in this volume are not there in the published *Diary,* but there are other differences that cannot be explained by simple expurgation. For example, during this incestuous romance, which the expurgated version treats as a simple "visit," there is a moment when some mail arrives.

The expurgated version has it this way: "When Samba the Negro brought the mail on a silver platter, my father said, 'Take them away. We have no need of anyone in the world'" (1994, 238). *Incest* tells it this way: "When the servant presented the mail and Father saw letters for me, he said, 'Am I going to be jealous of your letters, too?'" (214). The expurgated version includes things left out of the unexpurgated (Samba the Negro and the silver platter), and the unexpurgated represents Nin's father's statement as a jealous one rather than a romantic one. There is a formal or textual monstrosity here, that has nothing to do, really, with the expurgation of sensational material and everything to do with the essential shapelessness of this textual material, which refuses to recount a single version of the events it purports to be recording from life.

There is also, to be sure, a monstrosity of content here — or perhaps what might better be called a monstrosity of presentation, in which both what is narrated and how it is narrated contribute to the monstrous quality. That is, Nin here offers us a story of events supposed to be culturally horrifying — a lovingly detailed sexual encounter between father and daughter — presented in language much more polite than that used by Henry Miller in a moment of metaphysical musing. This monstrosity is essentially personal. It concerns private life. But Nin insists on recording it, meaning ultimately to publish it in some form or other. Uttering the unspeakable in prose that is neither brutal nor vulgar: that is Nin's way. But there are ramifications to Nin's project that will have to be followed out with some patience if we are to understand the monstrous richness of her enterprise. Without claiming to follow all of these pathways, or even to have traced one from root to blossom, I will try to do some justice to two of the aspects of monstrosity in Nin's text. One of these becomes plainer as the diary approaches the beginning of World War II. This same process is visible in Virginia Woolf's writing during the same years, both in her published books and in her diaries. What is striking when their diaries are looked at together is that, despite their enormous differences, Woolf and Nin share certain feelings about gender and about their roles as women writing in what had been — and was still in many important respects — a man's world. In particular, both saw the war as a product of masculine madness.

To understand Nin's view of her world's monstrosity, we shall have to follow her attempts to distinguish it from Henry Miller's masculine view. In volume 1 of *The Diary*, Nin wrote of Miller: "He carries one vision of the world as monstrous, and I carry mine. They oppose each other and also complement each other" (58). "One" vision, not "a" vision — indicating that there are two different visions of the world as monstrous: Miller's male one and Nin's female one. The diary itself is mentioned so often in the diary that it becomes almost a character. Miller suggested that "the diary may die," but Nin replied: "Why should it? I am afraid to forget. I do not want to forget anything" (117–18). Nin worried that Miller suffered from "a monstrous growth of the ego" (131), and she observed that "he runs from extremes of sentimentality to cold, monstrous madness" (166). But the madness of the world itself began to impress her when she moved to the Cité Universitaire to study psychoanalysis at the urging of Otto Rank in June of 1934.

While at the Cité Universitaire, I experienced my first knowledge of the monstrous reality *outside*, out in the world, the cause of D. H. Lawrence's and Henry's ravings and railings on the disintegration of the world. Doom! Historical and political. Pessimism. Suicide. The concrete anxieties of men losing power and money. That I learned at the School! I saw the headlines, I saw families broken apart by economic dramas, I saw the exodus of Americans, the changes and havocs brought on by world conditions. Individual lives shaken, poisoned, altered. (1994, 331)

But there are also moments when she doubts the reality of this external monster: "All life suddenly looks monstrous again, and yet is it a monster?" There are days when she can laugh and "doubt the monster, its presence, its reality" and suspect that it "is only a nightmare" (1974, 182). Events, however, conspire to persuade her that the monster is real. In March 1938 she writes, "*Hitler has marched into Austria*. Franco is encircling Barcelona, and France, afraid of war, is not coming to its help. . . . When the world becomes monstrous and commits crimes I cannot prevent, I always react with the assertion that there is a world outside. . . . All that is happening is monstrous. But how does one fight such a monster?" (302, Nin's emphasis). Virginia Woolf was asking the same question a few months later. Her nephew Julian Bell had been killed in Spain in 1937. In August 1938 she wrote these lines: "Hitler has his million men now under arms. . . . Harold . . . hints it may be war. That is the complete ruin not only of civilization, in Europe, but of our last lap. Quentin [her other nephew] conscripted &c. One ceases to think about it — that's all. . . . What else can a gnat on a blade of grass do?" (162).

That sense of powerlessness as the public sphere intrudes into private life pushes the diaries of the time to extremes. Woolf and her Jewish husband contemplated a possible invasion of England by the Nazis in 1940: "This morning we discussed suicide if Hitler lands. Jews beaten up. What point in waiting? Better shut the garage doors" (284). The war, Woolf suggests, has affected her as a person by the threat of violence, but it has also affected her and other writers as writers by taking away their audience: "No echo comes back. I have no surroundings. I have so little sense of a public" (299). One answer to this situation, the answer adopted by Nin and Woolf, was to give the diary more energy, where no echo was needed. Stevie Smith put it this way in a letter: "Yes, our times are difficult but our weapon is not argument I think but silence & a sort of self-interest, observation & documentation (I was going to say 'not for publication' but I am hardly in a position to say that!)" (Smith 258). Another answer, that adopted by George Orwell and Rebecca West, was to move from fiction, which they both had written with some success, to the monstrous personal chronicle, hoping, as Orwell indicated at the end of *Homage to Catalonia*, to rouse his audience from "the deep, deep sleep of England, from which I sometimes fear that we shall never wake till we are jerked out of it by the roar of bombs" (232).

West's attempt to awaken England took the form of a chronicle describing a trip to Yugoslavia, which was also a trip back in time to the roots of the coming war and the recently past war in the imperial projects of ancient

and modern times, and especially in those epochs of imperial decline, which she called, speaking of the assassination of the Austrian archduke and his wife at Sarajevo
that began World War I, "the monstrous frailty of empires" (179). For West, as for Nin and Woolf, the monstrosity of the world was a gendered monstrosity. That
is, men were largely responsible for it — and not just men
in themselves but what West called "education with a
masculine bias." In Salonae, she saw little girls being
taught by nuns ("women who have accepted the masculine view of themselves"), who she feared were "instill-
ing into their charges some monstrous male rubbish"
(163). For West, however, there were two forms of monstrosity — a male and a female form. Asked by a hospital
nurse why she thought the assassination of the king of
Yugoslavia (in 1937) was terrible, she thought about the
difference between men and women this way: "Her
question made me remember that the word 'idiot' comes
from a Greek root meaning private person. Idiocy is the
female defect: intent on their private lives, women follow
their fate through a darkness deep as that cast by mal-
formed cells in the brain. It is no worse than the male defect, which is lunacy: they are so obsessed by public af-
fairs that they see the world as by moonlight, which
shows the outlines of every object but not the details in-
dicative of their nature" (3). In *Black Lamb and Grey Falcon* West tried to combine the virtues of both these defects, producing an androgynous monster of a text,
chronicling the monstrous history that had made the
coming war inevitable. She saw this in specific events
and particular places, ranging from the incredible butch-
ery of the archduke Franz Ferdinand's hunting adventures ("the half million beasts which had fallen to Franz

Ferdinand's gun by his own calculations" [335]) to the "monstrous indecency" of the German war memorial at Bitolj (762), and she saw it in the doctrine of Christianity itself: "This monstrous theory that supposes that God was angry with man for his sins and that he wanted to punish him for these . . . and that he allowed Christ to suffer this pain instead of man and thereafter was willing on certain terms to treat man as if he had not committed these sins" (828).

The grey falcon of West's title comes from a Serbian epic about their conquest by the Turks, in which their leader, visited by the Holy Spirit in the form of a falcon, accepts a heavenly kingdom at the cost of losing the crucial battle. The black lamb is a blood sacrifice in a pagan ritual still performed in the Serbia of 1938. In the epilogue to her book, West expresses her fear that England will make the monstrous choice of defeat and enslavement:

> Again the grey falcon had flown from Jerusalem, and it was to be with the English as it was with the Christian Slavs; the nation was to have its throat cut as if it were a black lamb in the arms of a pagan priest. We were back at the rock. We were in the power of an abominable fantasy which pretends that bloodshed is peculiarly pleasing to God, that an act of cruelty to a helpless victim brings down favour and happiness on earth. We, like the Slavs of Kossovo, had come to a stage when that fantasy becomes a compulsion to suicide. For we had developed enough sensibility to know that to be cruel is vile, and

therefore we could not wish to be the priest whose knife made the blood spurt from the black lamb's throat, and since we still believed the blood sacrifice to be necessary, we were left with no choice, if we desired a part in the service of the good, but to be the black lamb. (1121–22)

Finally, as she brings her epilogue to a close, she rejoices in the coming into power of Winston Churchill, "who cannot be imagined as wanting to die, though he would die if a more liberal allowance of life were to be released by his death," and she adds, "It was good to take up one's courage again and feel how comfortably it fitted into the hand" (1125).

Finally, having said all this, it should be added that West's androgynous intention is to drive her personal chronicle well inside the boundaries of history itself. Stevie Smith had said, "Our weapon is not argument . . . but . . . observation & documentation." But West's weapons are personal observation and documentation put in the service of an argument about the folly of empire and empires, from Alexander the Great to Hitler, not excluding the British Empire itself. It was no accident that she chose the image of a woman chronicling the fall of the Roman Empire in describing her own motivation. Above all, West castigates "the inability of empires to produce men who are able both to conquer territory and to administer it" (1092). And she drives this indictment home with a wide-ranging and richly informed discussion of the Roman and Ottoman Empires. It is an extraordinary achievement, which has never received its due because it fits into no academic niche, no literary genre. What I have been calling the monstrous personal chronicle is not exactly a genre either, but only a provisional way of looking at certain major texts that have suffered in exactly this way, being undervalued because literary critics have failed to produce a scaffolding from which to examine them. Modernist critics have found ways of domesticating such monsters as *Ulysses* ("spatial form," "the mythic method") and *The Cantos* ("a poem including history," "a modern epic") but have been less assiduous in their examination of other, more overtly personal, monstrous texts. It is time, I am suggesting, to use a framework like the monstrous personal chronicle to bring these works together.

Many writers between the two world wars felt the same concerns and responded in similar ways — by asserting themselves, even as they tried to leave some testimony to the other lives around them. This impulse, in monstrous times, resulted in the generation of monstrous personal chronicles. We need, I think, to reconsider this time and its literary culture, putting what Miller called these "chronological tapestries" at the center of our investigations. If we can do so with sufficient generosity of spirit and critical acumen, we shall find our notions of modernity and the modern forms of narrative changing as we read. We will understand this part of our cultural heritage more adequately — and perhaps even arrive at a clearer sense of what we are in our own time and how we came to be this way.

Light Reading

The Private-Eye Novel as a Genre

After a few months' reading it suddenly dawned on me that the detective novel had its own peculiar technique and its own unique appeal, and that it operated according to its own individual rules — in short, that it constituted a *genre* of literary entertainment quite distinct from every other class of fiction.

W. H. Wright, "S. S. Van Dine"

But down these mean streets a man must go who is not himself mean, who is neither tarnished nor afraid. The detective in this kind of story must be such a man.

Raymond Chandler

My whole intent in this book is to connect the ordinary with the extraordinary: the humble text with the exalted text, the sacred with the profane, the common reader with the uncommon writer, and the common writer with the uncommon reader. As a teacher I have for years seen a major part of my task as helping students to see reading as a craft, a set of methods or practices that can be learned, a skill that can be improved by anyone willing to make an effort, though it can never be entirely

[138]

mastered by any person, however gifted and dedicated. A large part of the craft of reading is the ability to "place" or "situate" any particular text, both provisionally, as a way to begin a reading, and more firmly, as the reader's reading leads to correction of that provisional view. This is something we all do automatically in our ordinary exchanges with other human beings. Sometimes people say things that puzzle us, and we ask ourselves, "Where is he coming from?" — which means, roughly, Why is he saying that? or What's behind that utterance? My point is that we do this all the time, and that we think of it, even colloquially, as placing or situating — we think in terms of "Where?" and "from."

To situate a text is, among other things, to locate it in time and place, to know where it is coming from. I remember vividly an experience I had forty years ago, during my early days as a teacher, when my department gave an examination to a large group of students — a test on which they were asked to respond critically to a variety of poems that we presented, as I. A. Richards and the New Critics had encouraged us to do, without any background information at all: just the poems, minus the names of their authors. One student was very severe on one of our chosen poems, condemning it for using an affected poetic style completely unsuitable for a modern poet. This student, who has since won a Pulitzer Prize for poetry, was absolutely right. The poem was by William Shakespeare. Having read it as a modern poem, the student found it affected and inauthentic. It was a problem in situating the text, which we examiners had caused by concealing the author's name. Read as a sixteenth-century sonnet, it was both typical and a strong example of the type. Read as a modern poem it failed —

and in particular failed to be modern. By cutting the poem off from its situation, we had produced a bad test, because the situation is part of the poem, part of the cultural text out of which particular poems emerge. I never forgot that lesson.

In the normal world (as opposed to the world of testing) we encounter most texts along with clues about their sources. Written utterances differ from oral ones in the degree to which they are separated from those who originated them, though, as Jacques Derrida has elaborately shown, this estrangement is always a part of any utterance or speech act. It will be worth pausing to consider the implications of this. When a familiar person speaks to us in a familiar idiom, we have a low degree of separation — virtually no problem in situating the text — but since we never know anyone (even ourselves) perfectly, we never reach the zero degree that would mean perfect understanding. Even the heroes of Homer, in their interior monologues, find themselves asking, "alla ti e moi tauta philos dielexato thymos," "why does my dear heart [or, actually, liver, *philos thymos*] argue with me this way?" (see Scholes and Kellogg 179) — indicating that their selves are divided into disputing parts, and that one part does not know the motives of the other. The complexities of communication would be unbearable if we did not have all sorts of crafty ways of cutting through them. In the case of literary texts a major way of managing these complexities — for both writers and readers — is by placement according to type or genus, for which we awkwardly use the French word *genre*.

In current critical speech, however, the word has two rather different significations. One is simply a reference to the type of any given work. In this sense "epic" and "novel" are genres. But we also use the word in a way more loaded with values. In this second sense we speak, rather contemptuously sometimes, of "genre fiction" as of a lower order of literary production. In this sense *genre* means formula, a way of cranking out virtually identical texts to serve a culturally debased group of readers: think Westerns, Harlequin Romances, sitcoms. The formulaic quality of these texts can be thought of as indicating a very low level of craft, totally devoid of art. Without challenging this characterization directly, I would like to complicate the issue a bit. I believe that genre fiction is sometimes practiced at a very high level of craft, a level that brings it well within the range of what we normally think of as written art or "literature." If the genre of private-eye fiction belongs in the category of crafty fiction, as I believe it does, the inclusion of the works of Raymond Chandler among the classics published by the Library of America is a clear case of work in this genre achieving a position of canonicity in American literature. And one can easily think of works in other categories, such as certain Western novels and films, that transcend the supposed limits of genre fiction.

It is possible, I believe, for works in the upper reaches of high literature to become so literary that they move beyond the level of readability for most literate people (as is surely the case with Joyce's *Finnegans Wake*, for example). But in this essay, as in others in this book, I am more interested in the opposite side of the problem. That is, I am interested in exploring the lower border between art fiction and genre fiction. In particular, I want to look at the way a "new" genre comes into being, how its generic qualities become established as norms for this particular craft, and how it is possible for certain works in an established genre to attain a high level of achievement while still exhibiting all the stigmata of their crafty origin. I shall also be arguing that readers familiar with the established patterns of a genre will be in the best position to enjoy the achievements of the strongest work produced using those patterns — arguing that crafty readers will get the most from works that push craft to the level of art.

Our present notion of art is rooted in the Italian Renaissance and is elaborately intertwined with the rise of capitalism and individualism. The wealth of banking families like the Medici supported and rewarded the individualization that made crafts into arts in Renaissance Florence and other Italian city-states. This process (richly documented and vigorously narrated by Jacob Burckhardt in *Civilization of the Renaissance in Italy* [1860]) led inexorably to an emphasis on genius and masterpieces, which still guides much of our thinking about school curricula today. Literature followed the visual arts through this process, with poetry leading the way. It was not until late in the nineteenth century that fiction attained the status of an art — a status that was based on an invidious distinction between art and craft, between the artist who innovates and the crafty artisan, who simply repeats what has been done before. The prestige accorded innovation, under this regime of art, made avant-gardism an essential aspect of works claiming to be "modern." But the excesses of avant-gardism led even the most exalted of modernist writers to keep reminding their fellows about the necessity of being good at their craft. Both Pound and Eliot, for example, stressed knowledge of the poetic tradition as a crucial matter for readers and for writers as well. If I assert that good craft is better than bad art, then, I feel that I am working within that modernist tradition myself, though my emphases, shaped as they are by our current cultural situation, are somewhat different. And that is indeed what I want to assert: that writers of a crafty genre like the private-eye novel are more rewarding to read than many writers with greater pretensions to individual genius. To accomplish this task, however, I shall have to begin by discussing the notion of genre itself and its relation to patterns and formulae.

What is a literary genre? It is a sort of template, used by both writers and readers, to allow for relatively rapid composition and comprehension. That is, a writer composing a text in a recognized genre begins with a template, a preexisting form, that leaves certain blanks to be filled in. Some of these templates, as in the rules provided to aspiring authors by Harlequin Romances, are highly specific and leave very little to the imagination of those authors. They also provide readers with a very specific sort of textual pleasure that is minimally literary in the sense that it is based mainly on recognition of the familiar and requires hardly any cognition, or new thought, at all. When the word *literature* entered critical discourse as an evaluative term, around the beginning of the nineteenth century, it included a higher evaluation of newness or ingenuity than had prevailed before that time. The formal study of the arts that we call aesthetics was invented and developed only at the end of the eighteenth century. The new signification of "literature," as a name for certain superior texts, was applied within that framework. It went along with discussions of "taste" and, especially in discussing poetry, with a distinction, imported from Germany by Coleridge, between a lower sort of text dominated by a faculty called fancy, which could only manipulate concepts and images that were already in use, and a higher faculty called imagination, which could claim a share of the divine process by which the world had been created.

From that sort of formulation, which we call Romantic, evolved the modern form of avant-gardism, in which the divine pretensions were dropped but the creative capacity of imagination was given secular status as the ability to "make it new," or create new forms of textuality. This reached an extreme in postimpressionism, surrealism, cubism, and other modernist modes of textual production in all the arts. Along with it, inevitably, came the tendency to despise the formulae of craft — which led, as I have already indicated, to such back-formations as the arts-and-crafts movement, Bloomsbury's Omega Workshops, and injunctions like Yeats's "Irish poets learn your trade, / Sing whatever is well made" (Yeats, "Under Ben Bulben," 343) and Pound's "poetry should be written at least as well as prose" (Pound 371). The more academic formulations of the modernist imperative, as I tried to show in the first essay of this book, often took a less generous view of craft than the poets themselves, leaning too heavily on the supposed difference between fancy and imagination, or attacking "the fallacy of communication" in poetry. This sort of attitude made it difficult for writers who worked mainly at the level of craft to attain a proper level of recognition. That some of them have achieved such recognition, despite the odds, can serve as confirmation of the literary quality of certain works that took shape mainly under the sign of craft.

Because craft, in the area I am considering, is mainly designated by the term *genre fiction*, I am basing this discussion on the treatment of genre itself. The rise of the private-eye novel in America is a fascinating case of a recognizable genre coming into existence where one did not exist before. For this reason and others, this textual event can be used to develop the generic aspect of the reader's craft as well. I am going to simplify this complex process by arguing that the whole event can be traced through an examination of the work of three writers: Dashiell Hammett, Raymond Chandler, and Ross Macdonald. Before turning to the specific details of their texts, however, I must ask the reader to bear with me while I elaborate some basic features of the theory of genres and complicate this a bit by some discussion of the theory of styles or modes of expression. I will make it as brief — and as clear — as I can. In doing so I shall be going over ground that I covered some years ago in another book (1974), but I hope that the result will justify this.

On the theory of genres I have never found a better guide than Claudio Guillén, who presented in *Literature as System* (1971) a cogent discussion of the working of genres with particular application to his own special interest, the picaresque novel. Guillén noted that genres are both persistent, because they have been tested and found to work, and transitory, in that "they evolve, fade, or are replaced" (121). We shall be looking mainly at the evolution of a new genre in this essay. To discuss evolution in a literary genre, however, we need more than a theory of genre; we need a theory of styles or modes of expression as well. Theories of this sort began to appear in the eighteenth century, as in this formulation by Joseph Priestley: "The progress of human life in general is from poverty to riches, and from riches to luxury, and ruin. . . . Our very *dress* is at first plain and awkward, then easy and elegant, and lastly downright fantastical. Stages of a similar nature may be observed in the progress of all human arts" (173). More exact formulations of this sort, applied to the various human arts, have developed over time. For our purposes one of the most useful of these was presented by the French art historian Henri Focillon in his book *La Vie des formes*, translated as *The Life of Forms in Art* and reprinted in 1989. Focillon argued that art — always and everywhere — passed through similar stages, driven by an almost biological necessity. In his theory, which I will appropriate here for my own purposes, the stages in the evolution of artistic forms are these: "the experimental age, the classic age, the age of refinement, the baroque age" (52).

By combining Guillén's theory of genres with Focillon's theory of formal evolution, we will have the basic tools we need to begin a study of the rise of the private-eye novel. With a few more borrowings from structuralist and semiotic thinkers, which I shall introduce as necessary, we can complete our toolbox. Let us begin, then, by thinking about the formal qualities we all recognize as typical of the genre. All this must be provisional, of course, but we can start by trying to list the principal features of the genre, as we understand them from our casual reading of texts we can readily assign to this category. Guillén, working with the picaresque novel, notes that these formal qualities function not as a set of necessary requirements but as the elements of what Wittgenstein defined as "family resemblance" — that is, the features detectable in portraits of a single family made over generations, in which the "same" nose appears regularly, along with other features, but one does not need to find that nose, or any other single feature, in order to identify any one portrait as belonging to the family. One needs only a sufficient number out of the full set of qualities. As a way of beginning, I am going to set down Guillén's features of the picaresque, looking, in each case, for an equivalent in the private-eye novel, using the dagger (†) for the picaresque entry and a spade (♠) for the private-eye equivalent.

† The picaro is an orphan, a "half-outsider," an unfortunate traveler, an old adolescent.

♠ The private eye is a man who is not himself mean but goes down mean streets.

† The novel is in the form of a pseudoautobiography, narrated by the picaro.

♠ The novel is in the form of a case or set of cases, usually presented by a particular client, narrated by the detective.

† The narrator's view is partial and prejudiced.

♠ The narrator's view is limited but reliable.

† The narrator is a learner, an observer, who puts the world to the test.

♠ The narrator is a seeker for truth and justice in a world that often wants neither.

† The material level of existence is stressed — subsistence, hunger, money.

♠ Crime and its motivations are stressed.

† The picaro observes a number of conditions of life.

♠ The private eye encounters a broad range of the social and economic scale, from quite high to very low.

† The picaro moves horizontally through the geographical world and vertically through the social.

♠ The private eye does not change his own social status, which is somewhere between working class and middle class, and tends to be localized in a particular urban setting, a real (Los Angeles) or fictional (Personville) city.

† The episodes are loosely strung together, enchained rather than embedded.

♠ The episodes are enchained, but the links are tightly organized by the detective's pursuit of a solution to the case.

Guillén's features of the picaresque combine formal qualities, such as narration by the picaro, with aspects of the represented world, such as stress on the material level of existence. A similar combination allows us to generate a fairly clear preliminary notion of the private-eye novel as a genre. The two genres, I should think, have a more than casual affinity, in that both present readers with insight into a world that they would not wish to inhabit themselves — or perhaps with aspects of the world they do inhabit that they prefer not to experience directly. There is a little frisson for the reader who follows vicariously the often brutal events provided by both of these fictional genres. But the comparison to picaresque also allows us to get a firmer grip on the unique features of the newer genre. Historically speaking, the private-eye novel is a specifically American mutation of a form that emerged in the nineteenth century, after experiments by

Poe, Balzac, Wilkie Collins, and others, reaching something like a classical norm in the adventures of Sherlock Holmes and his followers. Reading this historical body of material while recovering from a long illness, Willard Huntington Wright arrived at the conclusion quoted in this essay's epigraph, and then transformed himself into S. S. Van Dine, a writer of best-selling detective novels, starting with *The Benson Murder Case* in 1928.

Van Dine not only discovered that detective fiction was "a *genre* of literary entertainment" (Van Dine 1936, 7–8), as he put it; he also decided, somewhat later, that he could formulate a set of "Twenty Rules for Writing Detective Stories" (74–81). Van Dine's detective, Philo Vance, was very much in the Sherlock Holmes tradition, transplanted from London to New York. Outfitted with a monocle, cigarette holder, and goatee, he was an elegant amateur, with wide but esoteric learning, who made the local police seem dull-witted and slow: in short, a descendant of Holmes and a relative of Ellery Queen and Lord Peter Wimsey. Basil Rathbone, who played Holmes so often on the screen, also played Philo Vance. It is not my intent here to follow this path and describe the genre whose formulae Van Dine tabulated so thoroughly but simply to indicate that it was mainly a British genre, dominated by figures like Holmes, and that American detectives like Queen and Vance seem oddly alien on American ground. They emerged from a northeastern culture that was strongly Anglophiliac, with an upper class, known simply as "society," that imitated the behavior of the British aristocracy as closely as possible.

The sort of "literary entertainment" described by Van Dine stressed the second of those words more heavily than the first. For him detective fiction was an elegant puzzle, "a kind of intellectual game," a "sporting event," in which the reader matched wits with the writer, who was required to "play fair with the reader." And he ruled out such things as "love interest," which, he believed, could only "clutter up a purely intellectual experience with irrelevant sentiment" (74). Van Dine understood his genre very well and gracefully accepted and performed the role of literary entertainer. Even so, the form as he practiced it was never quite Americanized. The monocle, the cigarette holder, the dressing gown or evening clothes — all these trappings of a certain social class were perhaps more essential to his enterprise than many readers understood. At the very least, this kind of fiction left a gap, a niche (to put it in the language of entrepreneurs), begging to be filled. The American private-eye novel grew into that niche. My task here is to show, as briefly as I can, how it grew.

S. S. Van Dine said that he had attended seven universities, including Harvard, where he met the man who became his editor, Maxwell Perkins of Scribner's, who is better known, perhaps, as the editor of some other writers. Dashiell Hammett, on the other hand, had one semester of high school at the Baltimore Polytechnic Institute, where the man who published his first writing — H. L. Mencken — had gone to school more than a dozen years earlier. Hammett was forced to drop out of school in 1908 to help in his father's small business, which was in difficulties (Layman 8). Mencken, incidentally, collaborated with W. H. Wright, long before Wright became S. S. Van Dine, on a travel book about the pleasures of certain European cities. Hammett's life was different. "At the age of twenty, in 1914, Dashiell had contracted gonorrhea; he was beginning to drink; he could not hold a job" (Layman 9). A year later he made a move that was to have a decisive effect on American literature: he joined Pinkerton's National Detective Agency, an organization of private detectives whose logo was a single staring eye. Since 1850 the Pinkertons had been filling a niche in American law enforcement, training "operatives" who could outperform local police forces in both the detection and the prevention of crime. The privatization of public functions is not new in this country.

By the time Hammett joined them, however, one of the Pinkertons' main functions was to break strikes, protect scabs, and bust unions. No one knows exactly how or when Dashiell Hammett was radicalized, but his time with this organization surely contributed to his understanding of how labor, management, and local politics really functioned in the United States. For our purposes, however, what is important is that he came to the writing of detective fiction from a background in private detection, which he drew upon readily and to great effect. He worked with the Pinkertons until 1922, taking a few years off to join the army during the war, and contracting the tuberculosis that was to dog him all his life. His first published story, "The Parthian Shot," appeared in H. L. Mencken and George Jean Nathan's *The Smart Set* in 1922, but he soon moved to the magazine Mencken and Nathan had founded in 1920 and then quickly sold, *Black Mask,* and in October of 1923 that magazine had the distinction of publishing the first story told by a short, fat, tough, and nameless gent, known only as a Continental Op — that is, an operative or employee of the Continental Detective Agency, Hammett's fictional version of the Pinkertons.

The voice of the Op struck a note that has remained

a major element in private-eye fiction ever since. Let us listen to it as Hammett fine-tuned it for the opening paragraph of his first published novel, *Red Harvest* (part in *Black Mask*, 1927; Knopf edition, 1929): "I first heard Personville called Poisonville by a red-haired mucker named Hickey Dewey in the Big Ship in Butte. He also called his shirt a shoit. I didn't think anything of what he had done to the city's name. Later I heard men who could manage their r's give it the same pronunciation. I still didn't see anything in it but the meaningless sort of humor that used to make richardsnary the thieves' word for dictionary. A few years later I went to Personville and learned better" (Hammett, *Red Harvest*, 3). A crafty reader should find a lot to ponder in this short paragraph. First of all, there is definitely a "voice" uttering these words, a personality that has chosen and arranged them. Secondly, the words themselves remind us to pay attention to voice, to locate a speaker by the way he pronounces — or fails to pronounce — his r's and the kind of vocalization he gives his vowels. There is a lot about language in this short passage, including the apparently casual reference to the dictionary. This is clearly what H. L. Mencken was going to call "The American Language" in his monumental study of the way we speak and write in this country. The sentences are short, the syntax direct, the grammar correct but not fussy. The speaker is better educated than Hickey Dewey, but he doesn't flourish that or claim literary erudition. What he does claim is a knowledge of people and places. He knows what a mucker is, and we respect him for it, whether we ourselves know or not. He knows about thieves' slang and has no respect for it, because it is meaningless. He remembers names, places, physical features. This language is not far from Hemingway's and this voice would not be inappropriate for a Hemingway character. It is tough, knowing, with a kind of understated wit.

A few paragraphs later, having described his arrival in Personville, the man we will know only as the Op describes the city and its police force:

> The city wasn't pretty. Most of its builders had gone in for gaudiness. Maybe they had been successful at first. Since then the smelters whose brick stacks stood up tall against a gloomy mountain to the south had yellow-smoked everything into uniform dinginess. The result was an ugly city of forty thousand people, set in an ugly notch between two ugly mountains that had been all dirtied up by mining. Spread over this was a grimy sky that looked as if it had come out of the smelters' stacks.
>
> The first policeman I saw needed a shave. The second had a couple of buttons off his shabby uniform. The third stood in the center of the city's main intersection — Broadway and Union Street — directing traffic, with a cigar in the corner of his mouth. After that I stopped checking them up. (3–4)

Going in for gaudiness is clearly not a good idea, in architecture or in prose. But the sloppiness of the first three policemen encountered by the Op is even worse, because it indicates that public law enforcement is either slack or corrupt — if not both. The Op's prose — which of course is Hammett's prose — is neither gaudy nor sloppy.

It can hammer home the word *ugly* three times in a single sentence, but it is imaginative enough to see the grimy sky as emerging from the stacks of an industrial power that has destroyed the natural beauty of the mountains and turned the city's buildings dingy. All this is accomplished deftly, economically, and without a single word that suggests sentimental piety. The descriptive terms used — *gloomy, grimy, shabby,* and *uniform dinginess* — come from the middle range of the American language, but they work together powerfully. This prose sounds like spoken English, but it is tighter and more efficient than most actual speech. And these paragraphs are loaded with value judgments but free of sermonizing. The sentences seem to come as naturally as breathing, but there is a subdued fire in their breath. A new way of writing detective fiction is being generated by this language. We need only contrast it with the contemporary work of S. S. Van Dine to realize just how different it is.

Here are the opening paragraphs of *The Benson Murder Case* (1928):

> It happened that, on the morning of the momentous June the fourteenth when the discovery of the murdered body of Alvin H. Benson created a sensation which, to this day, has not entirely died away, I had breakfasted with Philo Vance in his apartment. It was not unusual for me to share Vance's luncheons and dinners, but to have breakfast with him was something of an occasion. He was a late riser, and it was his habit to remain *incommunicado* until his midday meal. The reason for this early meeting was a matter of business — or,

rather, of aesthetics. On the afternoon of the previous day Vance had attended a preview of Vollard's collection of Cézanne water-colors at the Kessler Galleries, and having seen several pictures he particularly wanted, he had invited me to an early breakfast to give me instructions regarding their purchase. (Van Dine 1928, 1)

The narrator, who claims to be S. S. Van Dine, met Vance at Harvard and has now become his private attorney, giving up his regular law practice to do this. He is clearly a kind of Dr. Watson, just as Vance is a kind of Sherlock Holmes. Vance lives well. "His apartment in East Thirty-eighth Street — actually the two top floors of an old mansion, beautifully remodeled and in part rebuilt to secure spacious rooms and lofty ceilings — was filled, but not crowded, with rare specimens of oriental and occidental, ancient and modern, art" (7). Vance's holdings are then enumerated in lavish detail. He not only has a private lawyer on his staff. He also has "Currie, a rare old English servant, who acted as Vance's butler, valet, major-domo and, on occasions, specialty cook" (6). Vance is "an expert fencer," his "golf handicap was only three," he has played polo for the United States against England, and he is "one of the most unerring poker players I have ever seen." He is also "gifted with an instinctively accurate judgment of people" and has become an expert psychologist, partly through "courses under Münsterberg and William James" (11–12).

All this is so over-the-top that it verges on parody. Wright (I will use his real name to distinguish the author from his narrator), who had written books on Nietzsche and on modern painting before turning his hand to crime, was a self-conscious modernist, who constructed his detective deliberately, giving him an almost inhuman element of positivistic science: "Until we can approach all human problems . . . with the clinical aloofness and cynical contempt of a doctor examining a guinea-pig strapped to a board, we have little chance of getting at the truth," Vance is quoted as having remarked. He has a Nietzschean "contempt for inferiority of all kinds" (9). And when he speaks, his language and manner are impossibly British. When informed by his friend, the district attorney of New York, about the murder of someone in their own social set, Vance pauses, yawning, in his "dressing-gown and bed-room slippers" to ask the D.A.: "Why the haste, old dear? . . . The chap's dead, don't y'know; he can't possibly run away" (17). There is much more in this vein in *The Benson Murder Case*.

If we remember Joseph Priestley's view of the stages of human culture — "The progress of human life in general is from poverty to riches, and from riches to luxury, and ruin. . . . Our very *dress* is at first plain and awkward, then easy and elegant, and lastly downright fantastical" — we can see how closely Wright's presentation of Vance fits the category of luxury, or elegance, becoming so excessive as to be "fantastical." As a student of art history, W. H. Wright was well aware of the evolution of styles. As a student of detective fiction, he had formulated the rules of the genre before writing a word based on those rules. As a modernist, he knew that he had to "make it new." His response was to push the classic norms of the genre into a fantastical mode, which I shall call baroque, though in this case rococo might be even more appropriate. (Henri Focillon remarked that rococo style is simply the eighteenth century's version of baroque.) My point is that W. H. Wright and Dashiell Hammett, coming to this genre from very different angles, and with very different backgrounds, saw the same situation. That each was connected to Mencken in a different way and that both appeared in the pages of *The Smart Set* only serves to heighten their differences. And, certainly, they reacted to the situation in ways so clearly different as to teach us something about our craft as readers. Wright pushed the envelope of the existing form. Hammett picked it up and transplanted it, trying to transform it into something quite different in the different soil of the American language, but the connections to its heritage are still there and visible throughout his writings. The villain of *The Dain Curse,* for example, is a figure somewhat like Philo Vance himself.

In terms of the craft of reading and the theory of genres, I am using the Philo Vance novels as examples of a genre: the "puzzle" sort of detective fiction that had pretty well rigidified into a formula by the time that W. H. Wright adopted it as a writer and codified it as a critic or theoretician of the genre with his "Twenty Rules." Too much of a modernist to simply crank out formulaic texts, he pushed the form — and especially his detective Philo Vance — into the overwrought excesses of baroque. The crafty reader will read these novels prepared to enjoy those excesses. Such a reader will also see that there is not much room for development left in this particular direction. The form is nearly played out. In the same way, however, such readers should be able to see what Dashiell Hammett was trying to do, and they should understand both the extent and the limits of his achievement, for he developed all the important elements of the mutated novel of crime and detection — the American "hardboiled" detective story — without ever getting all of them together in a single book, though he came very close, so close that he made it easy for a gifted successor to perfect the new genre and establish its classic norms of form and content. That gifted successor, who was also the most crafty reader Hammett has ever had, was Raymond Chandler.

In a few pages of his powerful essay "The Simple Art of Murder" (Chandler 1995, 2: 977–92), Raymond Chandler said a number of important things about Hammett and the form of writing he developed — things that we should keep in mind as we consider the work of both writers. The following items, lifted from that essay, in Chandler's own words, are just the highlights.

- Hammett ... was one of a group ... who wrote or tried to write realistic mystery fiction. All literary movements are like this; some one individual is picked out to represent the whole movement. Hammett was the ace performer.

- A rather revolutionary debunking of the language and material of fiction had been going on for some time. . . . But Hammett applied it to the detective story, and this, because of its heavy crust of English gentility and American pseudo-gentility, was pretty hard to get moving.

- Hammett gave murder back to the people who commit it for reasons, not just to provide a corpse.

- All language begins with speech, and the speech of common men at that; but when it develops to the point of becoming a literary medium it only looks like speech.

- I believe this style, which does not belong to Hammett or to anybody else but is the American language ... can say things he did not know how to say or feel the need of saying.

- He was spare, frugal, hardboiled, but he did over and over again what only the best writers can ever do at all. He wrote scenes that seemed never to have been written before.

A crafty reader, indeed. Let us count some of the ways. I am, in fact, using Hammett, Chandler himself, and Ross Macdonald to represent a whole movement, just as I am using Van Dine to represent the genre against which that movement was reacting — that "heavy crust of English gentility and American pseudo-gentility." This new genre, the private-eye novel, was seen clearly by its foremost practitioner as a move away from the puzzle sort of plot (whodunit?) to a plot driven by motivation, by crimes committed for "reasons." It was also seen by him as sustained by a literary version of the American language, a style common to Hammett, Hemingway, and other American writers. He notes, furthermore, that more can be done with this language, implying — and rightly, I should say — that he might be doing some of the "more" himself. My focus in what follows here will be a little different from Chandler's, but I want to acknowledge my indebtedness to him as a critic of both the puzzle and the hardboiled forms of detective fiction, to say nothing of his being the writer who perfected the genre I am discussing. But now let us get back to Hammett and what he did and did not accomplish.

Just as he might have done more with the American language, Hammett might have done more with the new generic form he was developing. In the ordering of artistic styles developed by Henri Focillon, Hammett represents the primitive, experimental phase. This emerges most clearly if we consider his detective figures and their relation to the narration of the stories. Leaving aside the short pieces, screenplays, serializations, and curiosities like his cartoon strip with Alex Raymond, *Secret Agent X-9* (1934), the lineup of Hammett's novels looks like this:

- 1929 *Red Harvest*

- 1929 *The Dain Curse*

- 1930 *The Maltese Falcon*

- 1931 *The Glass Key*

- 1933 *The Thin Man*

The first two of these novels feature the Continental Op, as both detective and narrator. The Op is very close to being the kind of figure we recognize as the typical private eye — like Chandler's Marlowe or Macdonald's Archer — in that he is tough, honest, and driven by a desire to discover the truth. He also, and this is crucial, tells his own story, so that we come to know him through his narrative voice — the voice we heard in the opening paragraphs of *Red Harvest* quoted above. And he is "private" in the sense that he is not a policeman, not caught up in the system of corruption that is endemic in big-city police departments, as we know too well. But he is also not "private," in that he works for Continental, a sanitized if not idealized version of the Pinkertons. He is given marching orders by the company, though he often exceeds or ignores them. This makes him just a bit different from the classic private eye, who contracts with a client directly, and who is not backed up by a company that can send out more ops if necessary. The essential loneliness of the private eye is already there in the Op, but his membership in an organization works against this. The Op reports to "the Old Man" in San Francisco, who sees through his sanitized reports. *Red Harvest* ends with those reports: "They didn't fool the Old Man. He gave me merry hell" (216).

The first phase of a new style, as Focillon described it, is "experimental." And we can see Hammett reaching toward the ideal form, the form that would have real staying power in the world of letters, and never quite getting there. In *The Maltese Falcon* he almost had the thing completely in his grasp. Sam Spade is certainly the model for all who followed him. But Sam does not narrate the story of the Falcon. This book is narrated by a nameless figure whose prose at the start of the story has drifted from the powerful American speech of the Op back toward pseudogentility. Consider, for example, the opening paragraph:

> Samuel Spade's jaw was long and bony, his chin a jutting v under the more flexible v of his mouth. His nostrils curved back to make another, smaller, v. The v *motif* was picked up again by thickish brows rising out-

ward from twin creases above a hooked nose,
and his pale brown hair grew down — from
high flat temples — in a point on his forehead.
He looked rather pleasantly like a blond Satan. (3)

We are a long way from the Op's language here. Perhaps, when Chandler remarked that Hammett did not
realize all that might be done with American speech, he
was thinking that stuff like this could have been
avoided. The second Hollywood version of this story
(*Satan Met a Lady*, 1936), made by people who perhaps
did not read carefully beyond that opening paragraph,
portrayed Spade, complete with dressing gown and
pipe, as a chap not so different from Philo Vance. All one
can say is that this paragraph invited that abuse. Fortu-
nately, Hammett moved away from this narrative voice
in the course of the novel, which is a triumph, above all,
of dialogue. The resulting book was, in fact, just waiting
for the right director and the right cast to become a classic film, and along came John Huston in 1941, with
Humphrey Bogart, Mary Astor, Sidney Greenstreet, Peter Lorre, and others, to make it one. This film version,
which we remember so vividly, used that dialogue and
gave us Bogart in place of the "blond Satan" of Hammett's unfortunate opening.

My point is that Hammett, in his experiments, had
all the elements of the new form of detective fiction in his
grasp but did not put them together and hold them together. *The Glass Key* is a novel about politics and friend-
ship that seems hampered by its commitment to traditional detection. And *The Thin Man* gives us a boozy
ethnic version of Philo Vance at large in the speakeasies

of New York. He is a private individual, he detects, and he tells his own story, but he is some distance from both the Op and Sam Spade. It is ironic but fitting that the title, which referred to an important character in the novel, came to stand for the detective Nick Charles himself, in a series of films that fell into the classic "puzzle" mode, complete with all the suspects gathered in one room for the final revelation. Hammett was a true pioneer. He mapped the country but he did not cultivate it, or even, perhaps, realize what a rich and fruitful territory he had discovered. It remained for Raymond Chandler to do that.

Chandler was born in Chicago in 1888, six years before Hammett's birth in Baltimore. But he became a writer after Hammett, and Hammett was his great model. When his parents were divorced, he moved with his mother to England at the age of seven, and he later went to Dulwich College outside London, where he received a traditional education in the classics. It is perhaps worth noting that he attended Dulwich just after a boy who was to become an enormously successful writer of comic prose: P. G. Wodehouse. After Dulwich, Chandler tried many careers, ending up in the oil business in Los Angeles, until, in 1932, depressed over domestic difficulties and drinking heavily, he was fired and forced to consider another career. He turned to writing, discovered *Black Mask*, and published his first detective story there in 1933, the year in which Hammett's last novel appeared. Here is the list of Chandler's major novels, with their dates:

- 1939 *The Big Sleep*

- 1940 *Farewell, My Lovely*

- 1942 *The High Window*

- 1943 *The Lady in the Lake*

- 1949 *The Little Sister*

- 1954 *The Long Goodbye*

The six years between his first story and his first novel in this mode were not wasted. During that time he mastered his craft, coming to understand very well what Hammett had accomplished and what remained to be done. And then he did it. He wrote *The Big Sleep* in three months, but that was possible only because he was able to use stories he had already written, revising and connecting them in the process of constructing his novel. This is not the place to stop and analyze this work, but a careful study of his revisions is a lesson in the craft of writing that every crafty reader should consider. The stories he reworked in writing his novels have been collected with the title *Killer in the Rain*. It is a pity they are not in the Library of America volumes of Chandler's work, for we can learn a good deal about Chandler's craft by looking at the opening paragraphs of *The Big Sleep* and the source from which Chandler drew them. Here is the second paragraph of chapter 3 in "The Curtain," in which the detective, named Carmady, calls on the wealthy General Winslow:

> Oil paintings hung around me, mostly portraits. There were a couple of statues and several suits of time-darkened armor on pedestals of dark wood. High over the huge marble fireplace hung two bullet-torn — or

moth-eaten — cavalry pennants crossed in a glass case, and below them the painted likeness of a thin, spry-looking man with a black beard and mustachios and full regimentals of about the time of the Mexican War. This might be General Dade Winslow's father. The general himself, though pretty ancient, couldn't be quite that old. (Chandler 1980, 93)

This scene was rewritten by Chandler as the opening of *The Big Sleep*. The rewrite elaborates the scene extensively, and we shall look at that. But first let us consider the opening paragraph, in which Chandler allows his detective to introduce himself. He has in mind, I believe, not his own previous work here, but the opening paragraph of *The Maltese Falcon*, in which Hammett presented Sam Spade as a "blond Satan." That is, he understands that a description of the private eye is a good way to begin this kind of novel, but he also wants to use the occasion to let us hear Marlowe's voice for the first time, to get our first sense of him as a character, not from an external description but from his own self-presentation.

It was about eleven o'clock in the morning, mid October, with the sun not shining and a look of hard wet rain in the clearness of the foothills. I was wearing my powder-blue suit, with dark blue shirt, tie and display handkerchief, black brogues, black wool socks with dark blue clocks on them. I was neat, clean, shaved and sober, and I didn't care who knew it. I was everything the well-dressed private detective ought to be. I was

calling on four million dollars. (Chandler
1995, 1: 389)

In the first sentence we get a lot of scene-setting information, along with a sense that we are getting it from
someone who is very aware of things around him. In the
second sentence we move from "It was" to "I was," and
the narrator's clothing is described in detail, down to the
clocks on his socks. The next three sentences also begin
with "I was." This is the kind of simple, repetitive sequence of declarative sentences that Hemingway — and
Hammett — used so effectively. When the description
turns to the bodily state of the narrator, a certain tone of
self-mockery is established. By announcing that he is
"sober," he informs us that this is not always the case,
suggesting that he may also be less neat and clean than at
the moment being described. The self-mockery continues in the next sentence, which also gives us the crucial
information about his profession that we lacked up to
this point. The notion of a "well-dressed private detective" has a built-in irony, of which Marlowe is clearly
aware. This outfit requires a special reason, which is
provided in the final sentence, with its deft metonymy
(dollars for rich person) in the final phrase.

Crafty readers will use these words well. Such
readers will recognize that the narrator's profession signals the genre of the text, which is a major aid in placing
it, and they will also register the tone of understated wit
and self-deprecation. This prose signals competence at
the level of the writing, and because the voice is that of
the detective, it supports the other evidence of his competence at his trade. This voice and this character — and
this author — know what they are doing. The crafty

reader will recognize the craft of the writer and relax into that attitude of alert receptivity which is best for reading this kind of text. The average reader — crafty or not — will not be able to compare the paragraphs that follow with those Chandler was reworking to compose his novel. But we can develop our reading craft by making just this comparison. Here are the second and fourth paragraphs from *The Big Sleep*. (The third, dealing mostly with grounds, outbuildings, and cars, is entirely new.)

> The main hallway of the Sternwood place was two stories high. Over the entrance doors, which would have let in a troop of Indian elephants, there was a broad stained-glass panel showing a knight in dark armor rescuing a lady who was tied to a tree and didn't have any clothes on but some very long and convenient hair. The knight had pushed the vizor of his helmet back to be sociable, and he was fiddling with the knots on the ropes that tied the lady to the tree and not getting anywhere. I stood there and thought that if I lived in the house, I would sooner or later have to climb up there and help him. He didn't seem to be really trying. . . .
>
> On the east side of the hall a free staircase, tile-paved, rose to a gallery with a wrought-iron railing and another piece of stained glass romance. Large hard chairs with rounded red plush seats were backed into the vacant spaces of the wall round about. They didn't look as if anybody had ever sat in them. In the middle of the west wall there was a big

empty fireplace with a brass screen in four hinged panels, and over the fireplace a marble mantel with cupids at the corners. Above the mantel there was a large oil portrait, and above the portrait, two bullet-torn or moth-eaten cavalry pennants in a glass frame. The portrait was a stiffly posed job of an officer in full regimentals of about the time of the Mexican war. The officer had a neat black imperial, black mustachios, hot hard coal-black eyes, and the general look of a man it would pay to get along with. I thought this might be General Sternwood's grandfather. It could hardly be the General himself, even though I had heard he was pretty far gone in years for a man with two daughters in the dangerous twenties. (1995 1: 589–90)

The vague decor of the original story, with its inappropriate suits of armor, has been replaced with much more specific details. Those empty suits have metamorphosed into the knight in the glass scene, who will become a recurring motif in the story as a figure for Marlowe himself, who rescues one of those Sternwood daughters unclothed and seems, at times, to be making no more progress on the case than the knight in the image. The portrait, now of a possible grandfather rather than the father of the current general, is not just "spry" in appearance but has the "hot hard coal-black eyes" that are the visual equivalents of the sternness that is now a part of the family name. This is not just elaboration of the original. Every new detail, including those chairs that look, to Marlowe, as if nobody "ever sat in them," is doing the work of characterization of the family, its fortune, and its life. And, of course, Marlowe's attitude toward these things is also being conveyed very clearly. He registers this wealth, and has dressed to call on it, but he waxes ironic about pieces of "stained glass romance" and unused chairs as a way of asserting his own independent perspective. The knight in the image has raised his vizor "to be sociable," as Marlowe puts it. Marlowe has dressed up for the same reason. He will belong neither to the mean streets down which Chandler will send him nor to the stately rooms of the extremely rich, but he will operate very well across the whole range of society.

The opening of Chandler's second novel, *Farewell, My Lovely,* just as carefully positions Marlowe near the other end of the social spectrum: "It was one of the mixed blocks on Central Avenue, the blocks that are not yet all negro" (1:767). This begins as abruptly as some of Hemingway's fiction, and, like *The Sun Also Rises,* it very quickly introduces us to an interesting character — in this case Moose Malloy, a huge man in a very loud suit, of whom Marlowe says, "Even on Central Avenue, not the quietest dressed street in the world, he looked about as inconspicuous as a tarantula on a slice of angel cake." Marlowe is pushing the Hemingway/Hammett style into something a bit more elaborate, introducing the comparisons and similes that give Marlowe his particular style. He later criticized Ross Macdonald for going too far in this direction, but he himself certainly took the first steps. Marlowe is more of a wisecracker than any Hammett detective, and because he is the narrator, many of his wisecracks exist for the reader's benefit alone, though he often generates the ire of the police and others with his sharp tongue. As he tells General Sternwood in that first interview, he was fired from the district attorney's staff, "for insubordination. I test very high on insubordination, General." The general responds, "I always did myself, sir" (595), and their relationship is established.

Having found in Hammett the essential elements of this new genre, Chandler simply perfected them, and made Marlowe as memorable a narrator as his namesake, the narrator of Joseph Conrad's *Heart of Darkness* and *Lord Jim*. Marlowe is just a little softer than Sam Spade, and his prose just a bit richer and more complex than that of the Continental Op. Marlowe doesn't have a "girl Friday" secretary like Spade. He is a loner like the Op, and like the Op and Spade he is capable of something like love, but he quite rightly does not see himself as good husband material — something borne out in the pages of Chandler's unfinished final novel, *Poodle Springs*. Taking everything he needed from Hammett, and enriching what he took just enough, Chandler established the classical form of the private-eye genre. He did not surpass Hammett, but he established the features of the genre so firmly that they have lasted for seventy years and more, and proved capable of all sorts of modification and development in the hands of others. These features are the ones I listed provisionally above and will now repeat here with some refinements generated by the intervening discussion (and without the comparisons to picaresque fiction).

♠ The private eye is a man who is not himself mean but goes down mean streets. The private eye is a seeker for truth and justice, in a world that often wants neither.

♠ The private-eye novel takes the form of a story about a case or set of cases, usually based on a contract with a particular client, narrated by the detective.

♠ The narrator's view is limited by his own perspective, which the reader shares, but is ultimately reliable. His prose is distinctly American, suited to his education and experience. It is tough but alive and witty.

♠ Crime and its motivations are the primary subject matter of the novel. Discovery and rectification are its driving forces.

♠ The private eye encounters a broad range of the social and economic scale, from quite high to very low, while remaining himself somewhere in the middle. He often has a bit of college education. Marlowe "went to college once and can still speak English if there's any demand for it. There isn't much in my trade" (1: 594).

♠ The private eye does not change his own social status, and tends to be localized in a particular urban setting, often a real city like Los Angeles.

♠ The episodes are organized by the detective's contracted mission or missions, as he goes out into the world following clues, interrogating people, until the contract is fulfilled or must be abandoned.

As I have indicated, these are the features of a "family resemblance" rather than aspects of a tight conceptual structure that requires all of them. We recognize a work as belonging to the genre if it has a significant number of these features. We also recognize deviations from these features as interesting clues to a new intention or the satisfaction of a new need. When the private eye becomes a woman, for example, crafty readers will be interested in noticing what other generic features go along with that change — and what features persist. I want to call Chandler's novel's classics of this form not because they are "better" than Hammett's but because they combined all these features and established the norms of the genre. They were thus all in place when Ross Macdonald came upon the scene.

Dashiell Hammett did not finish high school, though he picked up a lot of learning after he left school. Raymond Chandler went to Dulwich College but did not go on to university after that. Kenneth Millar, the man who became Ross Macdonald, graduated from the University of Western Ontario (1938) and ultimately received a Ph.D. from the University of Michigan (1952). There is a progression here in the amount of formal education that is worth noticing, though it would be wrong to make too much of it. Hammett and Chandler were as literate as they needed to be, and Chandler, in particular, got a sound classical training at Dulwich. The most crucial part of Macdonald's education as a writer came from reading Hammett and Chandler. He began publishing novels under his own name in 1944 but did not really find his way until, in his fifth book, he introduced a private detective named Lew Archer and changed his writing name to John Macdonald. (Archer, you will remember, was the name of Sam Spade's partner, whose murder is the major crime of *The Maltese Falcon*.) Under some pressure from John D. Macdonald, Millar changed his writing name a couple of times, finally arriving at Ross Macdonald. But the introduction of Archer, and his adoption of the genre established by Chandler, were the crucial moves in his development as a writer — except for what he added to the genre himself, which will be the major focus of our consideration here.

Born in 1915, a full generation after his two major predecessors, he was well aware of their work when he made his move to adopt the form they had perfected. Matthew J. Bruccoli, whose chronology of Macdonald's life I have followed in this brief account, defined "hard-boiled" writing as "realistic fiction with some or all of the following characteristics — objective viewpoint, impersonal tone, violent action, colloquial speech, tough characters, and understated style; usually, but not limited to, detective or crime fiction" (Bruccoli 19 n.). He, too, finds the move to Archer as narrator-observer crucial to Macdonald's development, providing "a distinctive voice or point of view" (18) that Macdonald's earlier attempts at hardboiled fiction had lacked. With Archer, the semi-detached observer-participant, comes the voice and the style that enables this crafty genre to rise to the level of art. It is the voice established by Hammett and Chandler as the norm for this kind of writing. As Macdonald put it in 1972, "Hammett was the first American writer to use the detective story for the purposes of a major novelist, to present a vision, blazing if disenchanted, of our lives. As a stylist he ranked among the best of his time, directly behind Hemingway and Fitzgerald" (quoted in Bruccoli 19). Macdonald's admiration of his two predecessors, however, was short of idolatry, and long before he wrote those words of praise, he had come to feel that he was extending the range of the genre he had inherited. As he observed in 1957 when he finished *The Doomsters*, his ninth Archer book, "Maybe we can find a better label than hardboiled, better sponsors than Hammett and Chandler. They're my masters, sure, but in ways that count to me and a lot of good readers I'd like to sell my books to, I'm beginning to trace concentric rings around those fine old primitives" (quoted in Bruccoli 55).

What Macdonald meant by "good readers" is very much what I mean by "crafty readers," and these crafty novels we are considering provide an excellent way for such readers to hone their skills. The crafty reader will notice, of course, that by calling Hammett and Chandler "fine old primitives," Macdonald has positioned them in a manner similar to the one I have been proposing, except that I have insisted that, while Hammett is indeed a fine primitive, Chandler is an example of classical balance, the perfection of the style. Nevertheless, I would agree that Macdonald was, as he says, "beginning to trace concentric rings" around his predecessors. It's just that I see those rings as signs of a move beyond riches to luxury, as Priestley put it, or beyond classic to mannerism and the baroque, in the language of Focillon. Macdonald wrote more than twenty Archer books, more private-eye novels than his two predecessors put together, but he started earlier than they did, and had better health and habits than theirs. He also, in 1956–57, underwent extensive psychotherapy. As he said in *Self-Portrait: Ceaselessly into the Past* (1981), "My half suppressed Canadian years, my whole childhood and youth, rose like a corpse from the bottom of the sea to confront me" (30). He tried to find a novelistic form for these experiences, to break out of the hardboiled detective form, but he could not do it. What he found, finally, was that the voice of Lew Archer and the structure of the detective story could be used as a vehicle for everything he felt and knew. He put much of this material into *The Galton Case* (1959) and continued to mine this source for the rest of his career.

The change that he made in the form was not so much stylistic as structural. Archer as a character and narrator had never been terribly different from Marlowe, though his language was a bit more ornate, a fact that Chandler picked up and commented on as early as 1949 in a letter to a James Sandoe, a librarian at the University of Colorado with whom he corresponded frequently, about *The Moving Target*. Noting that plot elements were borrowed from *The Big Sleep*, and a character from *The Thin Man*, but accepting that as more or less normal, Chandler then zeroed in on what he took to be the excessive ornateness of Macdonald's prose. He noted that "scenes are well handled" but was offended by "this pretentiousness of writing" that he found in a description of a car as "acned with rust" (quoted in MacShane 163–64). Chandler, of course, is not innocent of phrases designed to call attention to themselves, though he argued against them vigorously in this instance. But my point is that for better or worse, this ornate version of the hardboiled style was there from the beginning — before the Ph.D., before the psychotherapy, in the very first Archer novel — and that it is in fact an extension of a tendency already there in Chandler himself. As I have said, the important change that Macdonald made in this genre was not stylistic. It was a matter of structure and content, of plot and character.

When I taught a senior seminar in these three writers at Brown University in 1999, we finished by reading two early Archer novels by Macdonald followed by two late ones. The class found the first two to add nothing to the genre established by Chandler and to be excessively derivative of Chandler in particular. They began to wonder, in fact, why I had put Macdonald next to his great predecessors. Then we read *The Galton Case* (1959) and *The Underground Man* (1971) — and they knew why. In those novels, and the other novels after *The Galton Case*, Macdonald succeeded in taking the troubled structure of American families and the entrepreneurial greed that has played such a powerful role in building and shaping this country, and putting them together into generational narratives, in which the roots of crimes are not in the present generation but back in the deeper past. Chandler looked in this direction as early as *The Big Sleep*, as Marlowe gazed at the portrait of General Sternwood's grandfather, but his plot remained within the present generation. And Hammett had toyed with the concept in *The Dain Curse*, only to write the curse off as a decoy for sinister doings in the present. But Macdonald put family histories and the mysteries of paternity and maternity at the center of his novels. *The Underground Man* begins with Archer meeting a child, a boy, who helps him feed peanuts to blue jays, a fleeting moment of pseudopaternal behavior on Archer's part that involves him in a chain of crimes that are mainly internal to the interlinked families to which the victims and the guilty belong.

Macdonald was certain he had taken the genre into new territory, and the critics, led by Eudora Welty, began to agree and to treat his novels seriously. The greed and lust, incest and exploitation presented in these novels, so richly interconnected with family histories, had all the drama and adventure for which the genre was noted, but the events were less remote from the experience of middle-class Americans, even though some of the families involved were quite rich. The sixties were the central decade for Macdonald's major period as a writer, and some of the concerns of the sixties — the generation gap, the destruction of the environment, and, to a lesser extent, race — are strongly there in the novels. *Sleeping Beauty* begins with an aerial view of an oil spill off the California coast:

> It lay on the blue water off Pacific Point in a free-form slick that seemed miles wide and many miles long. An offshore oil platform stood up out of its windward end like the metal handle of a dagger that had stabbed the world and made it spill black blood.
>
> The flight steward came along the aisle, making sure that we were ready to land. I asked him what had happened to the ocean. His hands and shoulders made a south-of-the-border gesture which alluded to the carelessness of Anglos. (1)

The environment and race are both introduced early here (these being the second and third paragraphs in the book), but the oil quickly leads Archer to a woman with family problems. When Roman Polanski made the film *Chinatown* in 1974, Macdonald's career was almost over, but Robert Towne's script, which won an Academy

Award, is a Ross Macdonald kind of story — a tangled web of incest, race, and the environment, driven by entrepreneurial greed and intrafamilial lust.

Ross Macdonald has also taken the basic repertory of characters he inherited and elaborated on that as well. The stock company that populates the Hammett/Chandler private-eye novel includes the following types:

- the eye-narrator (male, tough but honest, smart but fallible)

- the femme fatale (bad but sexually attractive for the eye)

- the girl Friday (good but not a sexual object for the eye)

- cops (friendly and unfriendly)

- the client (rich or poor, male or female)

- gangsters (male, more or less unfriendly)

- the victim or victims of crime (may be the client)

- the perpetrator (who may belong to one of the other categories as well)

What Ross Macdonald did with this stock company was to distribute all these roles (except the professional cops and gangsters) over the members of a family and often over more than one generation or through several interrelated families, so that most of the crimes are motivated by familial emotions carried too far, leading to incest or illegitimacy, producing children who grow up twisted by impossible demands. In these novels, with their longer time spans, the girl Friday may become a femme fatale, or the femme fatale become a doting mother or a bitter, lonely old woman — or both, like Mrs. Fredericks in *The Galton Case,* who must answer her son's question about why she lied for so long about his real father and why she lived with the man who killed her husband.

> "You got no call to judge me for doing that. It was to save your life that I married him. I saw him cut off your daddy's head with an ax, fill it with stones, and chunk it in the sea. He said that if I ever told a living soul, that he would kill you, too. You were just a tiny baby, but that wouldn't of stopped him. He held the bloody ax over your crib and made me swear to marry him and keep my lips shut forever. Which I have done until now."
>
> "Did you have to spend the rest of your life with him?"
>
> "That was my choice," she said. "For sixteen years I stood between you and him. Then you ran away and left me alone with him. I had nobody else left in my life excepting him. Do you understand what it's like to have nobody at all, son?" (241)

Here Macdonald shows how a femme fatale can become a mother and a mother's love give way to a more elemental emotion: the raw desire not to be alone in the world. In these short paragraphs we move from the violent world of hardboiled crime writing to something more powerful than lust or rage — and more ordinary. This is genre fiction pushing the envelope of the genre out-ward — in "concentric circles" as Macdonald said him-self — to great effect.

In terms of the critical categories I have been devel-oping here, I would say that the first Lew Archer novels were mannerist — just thin extensions of Chandler's style and subject matter, with certain features of the prose slightly exaggerated, so that Chandler himself was both-ered by them, almost as if he felt himself being parodied instead of merely pastiched. But the later Archer novels are truly baroque, the private-eye form caught up in Freudian tangles of an almost Theban sort and offering a glimpse beyond that, into existential anguish. This, in the words of Joseph Priestley, is "luxury and ruin." But not a literary or artistic disaster — far from it. The "luxury and ruin" are grounded in the world represented; the shape and style have merely expanded to accommodate them. And that is the essence of Macdonald's accom-plishment. He softened — and deepened — the form he inherited. But the form itself was sound and strongly rooted in its culture. We need not choose among these three writers. These are three powerful achievements in the craft of American fiction, and the genre that these writers established and elaborated has proved extraordi-narily durable and capable of modification.

The best of these original novels are all set in the Far West, whether the mountains of Poisonville or the cities of California. And Los Angeles — the very city of simulation, where oil and water, sex and gambling, farm-ing and filming mix to offer a heady brew of prizes and obsessions — Los Angeles proved to be the perfect, al-most indispensable location for these works. Many later fictions in this mode, right down to Elmore Leonard's

Get Shorty, have returned to that scene. But the form has also been moved to other cities all over North America, and detectives have changed in race, gender, and sexual orientation, so that the strain of homophobia so clearly visible in Hammett and Chandler has been triumphantly reversed in the novels of Joseph Hansen, for example, with his gay insurance detective, Dave Brandstetter. And Walter Mosley has produced powerful works going back over the Los Angeles of the Chandler/Macdonald period from the viewpoint of a black detective who must deal with racism and poverty as a routine part of his work. It has proved harder to transplant the private eye outside North America than it has been to change the race, sex, or orientation of the detective, and that is extremely interesting.

With a few notable exceptions, such as Dick Francis and Liza Cody in England, even the nontraditional or eccentric detective in Europe gets attached to the police. Nicholas Freeling's Van der Valk, for instance, and his later Castang, are policemen whose styles are unorthodox. Freeling is one of the many European writers who acknowledge their appreciation of and indebtedness to Chandler — in his case going so far as to use a title, *Not as Far as Velma,* that is lifted right out of the last sentence of *Farewell, My Lovely:* "It was a cool day and very clear. You could see a long way — but not as far as Velma" (1995 1: 984). The proliferation of works in this genre has been extraordinary, and these works have sustained an admirable level of craft for half a century since the genre first crystallized in Chandler's *Big Sleep* out of Hammett's earlier experiments. It has translated beautifully into film noir, too, even surviving, in the case of *Chinatown,* the move from stark black-and-white to rich colors.

Throughout aesthetic and cultural history, this is the way things have worked. At certain times, new steps have been taken that suited those times and places and were supported by those cultures, in terms both of financial rewards and of material to be shaped by a craft that could be learned and developed. The rise of private-eye novels as a literary genre, as a dialectical response to the decline of the genteel puzzle novel, and its development from primitive through classic and baroque versions, allowing for subsequent exportation and transformation — all this is a fascinating story in itself, but, for our purposes, it is also useful as a model of the way things regularly work in the world of arts and letters. That is why a study of the private-eye genre of fiction is extremely important for anyone who hopes to master the craft of reading.

Fantastic Reading

Science Fantasy as a Genre

I say again, if I cannot draw a horse, I will not write THIS
IS A HORSE under what I foolishly meant for one. Any key
to a work of imagination would be nearly, if not quite, as
absurd. The tale is there, not to hide, but to show; if it
show nothing at your window, do not open your door to it;
leave it out in the cold. To ask me to explain, is to say,
"Roses! Boil them, or we won't have them!" My tales may
not be roses, but I will not boil them.

George MacDonald

The first version, that of 1926, I believe: a carefully drawn
pipe, and underneath it (handwritten in a steady, pains-
taking, artificial script, a script from the convent, like that
found heading the notebooks of schoolboys, or on a black-
board after a lesson on things), this note: "This is not a pipe."

The other version. . . . The same pipe, same statement, same handwriting. But . . . the text and the figure
are set within a frame. The frame itself is placed upon an
easel, and the latter in turn upon the clearly visible slats of
the floor. Above everything, a pipe exactly like the one in
the picture but much larger.

Michel Foucault

My epigraphs are linked by their employment of a similar concept: a representation, an image, well or ill drawn, with a verbal caption that asserts or denies some linkage between the image and a category of reality. I find it interesting that the Victorian fantasist and the modern surrealist should hit upon the same formula for raising the question of reference and representation. Their differences are also instructive. The fantasist is mainly concerned with how to achieve the power of illusion, to generate authenticity for his illusion. The surrealist, on the other hand, progresses from questioning the status of images as illusions to questioning the status of reality itself. The fantasist, as we shall see, wants to create a second nature, a second culture, while the surrealist wants to deny the first nature, the first culture. In literature the Alice books of Charles Dodgson are dominated by a surrealist impulse. *The Lord of the Rings*, on the other hand, is a work of fantasy. I consider it an error for that admirable theoretician Eric Rabkin to have founded a theory of fantasy upon what I would call surrealism, just as I consider it an error for that perhaps even more admirable theoretician Tzvetan Todorov to have appropriated the word *fantasy* for what most of us would call the uncanny. Theoreticians, no matter how admirable, are often wrong, it would seem, but this is not a fault; it is their job, their duty, to be wrong so as to set the rest of us thinking about what might be right.

Having established myself as a nontheoretician, I shall now proceed to theorize, boiling a few roses and serving them up as a dish for the crafty reader. As the title of this essay proclaims, we are once again in the land of genre — my assumption being, here as elsewhere, that generic concepts help us clarify what we are doing as readers. In the present case, we are entering a field cluttered with such notions: fantasy, science fiction, speculative fabulation, and finally science fantasy. They are used not only by literary critics and theoreticians but even by the writers of dust jackets, from whom the crafty reader may often learn a lot — though not necessarily what the writer intended to convey. I read them all the time myself. You shudder with horror, no doubt, at my willingness to sink to such depths, but I can say in truth that on countless occasions the perusal of such ephemeral prose has spared me hours of anguish that I should have endured had I ventured beyond the jacket into the chaotic maunderings enclosed therein. In my experience at least half the time one does best to violate all proverbs, sayings, and other repositories of gnomic wisdom. Often one can, should, and does judge a book by its cover.

In this case, however, we are not judging a book but discussing an apparently curious and unnatural phenomenon: an oxymoronic monster named "science fantasy." A few lines from the land of blurbs and blushes will serve to launch us on our mission, which is nothing other than an attempt to determine the status — real or imaginary — of this purported creature. Here are the magic words: "a stunning blend of the lyric extravagance of fantasy and the keen edge of science fiction, meeting in a future so distant that it seems like the ancient past." In its stunning blend of confidence and vagueness this blurb might serve as cover for many works of science fantasy. If we don't look at it too closely, it even seems an accurate description of what we may find inside the book itself. These particular words served as a pitch for Gene Wolfe's *Shadow of the Torturer* (1980), the first volume of his *Book of the New Sun,* but they would be no less (and no more) appropriate for Samuel Delany's *Nevèrÿon* books and for many others.

If by "lyric extravagance" we mean language spinning discourse out of itself, words flowing from previous words, sounds echoing sounds, textuality rampant, semiosis unlimited, narrativity unbounded — well then, yes, these works are indeed characterized by "lyric extravagance," or "extra-vagance" as Thoreau liked to think of it. They are in principle interminable, affecting closure rather than effecting it. But what is the "keen edge of science fiction"? Obviously, it is meant to contrast with "lyric extravagance" on the principle of center and circumference or hard and soft — in some way to suggest by naming the extremes that *everything* has been included here.

Science fiction is described as hard and sharp — in contrast with the soft and shapeless lyric extravagance of fantasy. Science fantasy, then, is by definition an impossible object, hard and soft, pointed and uncircumscribed: a monstrosity. Yet it is said to exist. The existence of strange objects implies the strangeness of the world in which they exist. "Toto, I've a feeling we're not in Kansas anymore," says Dorothy in the film version of *The Wizard of Oz,* when the door of her hovel swings open upon a gang of Hollywood midgets in Technicolor. And she's right. She's in Los Angeles, the land of magical simulations and transformations.

But we are straying from our text. That blurby quotation concludes by asserting that Wolfe's narrative is set "in a future so distant that it seems like the ancient past." The assumptions behind this phrase are interesting. A whole theory of history is implicated in the syntactic structure governed by two little words: *so* and *that*. *So* far into the future *that* it resembles the ancient past. A notion of history as a cyclical pattern of possibilities presides over this utterance. At some point down the linear path of history, the scenery and decor will become familiar and humanity will be found organized in ways that are recognizable to us from the period of Western history extending from the Egyptian empire to the later Middle Ages, but with bits of modern science dropped into the mix. Faced with this pattern, which occurs in book after book, we are driven to ask certain questions. One which fascinates me is, Why not extend the cyclical future just a bit further until we reach the moment that resembles our own present time? What would a science fantasy set "in a future so distant that it seems like the present" actually be like? *Gravity's Rainbow*? *The Public Burning*? Such works certainly have their fantastic dimensions, but they present themselves as versions of our world rather than as other worlds. So, for that matter, do the Harry Potter books, which are set in our time but with a parallel world of magic coexisting with the world we know. We shall come to Harry's world later on. For the moment, however, I want to suggest that fantasy (plain fantasy, without the science) became a full-fledged literary genre only when it took as its central principle the construction of other worlds than ours. And this, in turn, could have happened only after we had begun to think of science as the only proper description of our world. Without science, no fantasy, because fantasy defines itself against science. Real folktales are not fantasy, however fantastic they may seem to us. They assume that this world, our world, includes magic and monsters. One question that needs to be answered, however, about the genres of fantasy and science fantasy, is why the new worlds that they propose to us seem always to bear some resemblance to our own ancient past.

This is by no means a simple question, nor can it be answered in a few words, but I would like to offer a hasty hypothesis about it. Whole worlds inhabited by sentient creatures take dimensions of development that no mind can encompass. No writer can invent an entire world. Thus every fictional world must borrow more than can be invented by its author. An understanding of human history enables a writer to think of one facet of a fictional world — say combat with swords — after which many other social, economic, and physical situations make themselves available as being culturally compatible with the chosen feature. Habits of information — what Umberto Eco calls the reader's "encyclopedia" — come to the aid of the fictional imagination, which could not function without them. The reader, crafty or not, furnishes a world to match the details supplied, but the crafty reader will be aware that this is going on — and will notice if the details provided are inadequate or contradictory. But the point is that only a few details from the historical past are necessary to start the reader on the task of furnishing a world appropriately.

Thus the past is always present in the futures of fantastic fiction. Why this past is so often a quasi-medieval one is a second question that we should consider. I believe that the medieval past dominates fantasy for a number of reasons. One obvious reason is that it presents a world in which magic fits comfortably, a world in which science had not yet made magic fantastic. A second reason is that fantasy has powerful generic links with both fairy tales and medieval romances. A third reason is ethical. Fantasy, until very recently, has always offered us a Manichean world in which values are polarized by absolutes of good and evil—a world especially compatible with the mixture of pagan and Christian beliefs prevalent in Europe in the Middle Ages. Fictions grounded in such a matrix regularly present ultimate good and ultimate evil embodied in the fictional characters of the text. It is this feature of modern fantasy more than any other that makes it anachronistic in our time. But we are getting prochronistic ourselves, and must turn to more basic questions of definition. If we are going to talk about science fantasy, we must at least consider the notions of science and fantasy themselves.

I do not believe that there are entities out there for which *fantasy* and *science* are simply the proper names. If we are going to discuss these notions, we shall have to begin by looking at the words themselves, rather than by trying to describe any changeless thing that might be named by such words. Let us begin with *fantasy*. This word has deep roots in ancient Greek culture. All of its modern meanings can be traced to these roots. Our present spelling of the word is based upon its Latinized transliteration. In Greek its initial letter is φ (phi). The Greek word *phantasia* is derived from the adjective *phanos* (meaning light and bright), the noun *phanos* (meaning torch), and the verb *phaino* (which means bring to light in the active and come to light or appear in the passive). The standard term in Greek philosophy for things that appear to the senses is *phainomena,* the neuter plural participial form of *phaino.* The Greek word *phantasia* is thus very closely related to *phainomena.* A *phainomenon* is a thing insofar as it appears to us. *Phainomena* are the visible or apprehendable aspects of things. A *phan-*

tasía, on the other hand, is a mental image, perhaps our recollection of the appearance of a thing, perhaps drawn from some other source.

In Aristotelian thought, the word *phantasía* also names the faculty by which things are imaged or imagined to be present. The word can also refer to a poet's ability to suggest the presence of things through images. Because this word was tied to appearances and imaginings, it was frequently used to refer to instances of imagination unaccompanied by presence: for hallucination, for exaggeration, for inauthenticity. If we can imagine the fortunes of this word in Greek history, we must see it as gradually being pushed from its connection with light, in which things may be seen as they actually are, to a more marginal position, pushed out by its opposition (in Aristotelian thought, especially) to other words like *doxa, episteme, nous, dianoia*. Its English cognates are *fancy* and *feign*. The English word *phenomenon* keeps its distance from fantasy by retaining a remnant of Greek spelling, the *phi* that justifies our use of *ph* in place of *f*. In the world of positive science, fantasy is Cinderella. But where is the prince in such a world?

The word *science* has another history altogether. The modern word has a clear pedigree going back to Latin, where it appears as *sciens* (knowing), the past participle of *scire* (to know or know how to). This word and its close relative *sciscere* (to investigate, inquire), with its participle *scitus* (clever, knowing), delineate clearly the path that the word *science* will follow: science as knowledge and science as technique or technology. In the medieval world God's knowledge could be called science. After Bacon and Newton the word came gradually to apply only to knowledge acquired by approved methods within an institutionally guaranteed empirical paradigm. Thus, for a thousand years and more, science has meant the best knowledge, the highest learning, by whatever standards were in place at the time. A lucky word, to have kept always what our blurb writer called its "keen edge." But why has the word no history before Rome? Why did it appear amid the grandeur of empire and technology rather than as a centerpiece in the glories of Greek art and — well — science?

The Greeks had plenty of words for knowledge, one of which, *gnosis*, gave Latin *cognoscere* (to get to know, and, in the perfect tense, to know, to recognize). The Latin *scire* may be a shortened form of *cognoscere* — though this is mere speculation on my part. But even if it is, it seems to have been attracted to and shaped by another cognate that Webster tells us is "akin" to *scire*. This other word is *scindere*: to cut, rend, split; to divide, separate. The Latin *scindere* does have a pedigree in Greek, deriving from *schízo:* to split, cleave, part, separate, or divide. The word in Greek was used to refer to logs, bodies, minds — anything that could be divided. Birds, whose wings were divided into feathers (unlike bats and beetles), were called *schizopteros* (split-winged). Splinters and chips of wood for kindling were called *schízes*. Everything from a division of opinion to a distinguishing feature of female anatomy could be called a *schísis*.

The linkage between *scindere* and *scire* in Latin justifies the banal metaphor of our contemporary blurb writer. Science fiction comes by its "keen edge" honestly, for science as knowledge has been intimately linked from its beginnings with splitting, dividing, dissecting in order to know. Fantasy, which began as knowledge of things from the way they present themselves to the senses as images, forms, appearances, has had to yield its place to science, which learns by taking things apart to see how they work. For centuries, the nonviolent knowing of fantasy has been displaced by the violent knowing of science. For centuries we have believed that the empirical knowledge called science was real knowledge, and the intuitive knowledge called fantasy was false knowledge. We have believed, in short, that science was science and fantasy was fantasy. Were we wrong? We could do no other than what we did. The interesting question is whether we are changing now. I propose to approach that question by looking at the literary genres that have been associated with science and with fantasy, and, finally, at this new hybrid, science fantasy.

The notion that fantasy is a literary genre, a subcategory of fiction like "gothic" or "picaresque," is an extremely recent arrival in the world of criticism. The many definitions of fantasy in such major tomes as the OED and *Webster's International* (second edition) do not include an entry defining fantasy as a fictional genre. Most critical studies of narrative literature produced in this century have no index entry for fantasy. Even the wise and witty E. M. Forster, in *Aspects of the Novel,* made a hopeless botch of his chapter on fantasy, calling *Tristram Shandy* "the greatest of them" (Forster 111) and insisting that Joyce's *Ulysses* belonged in this category because "the raging of Joyce . . . seems fantastic" (123). These atrocities in a book which was in many ways so astute are quite startling, but they document a state of incomprehension that extended well beyond the confines of Cambridge and Bloomsbury. Fantasy was not perceived as a fictional genre until quite recently. This or that element in a work might be called fantastic, but the concept of a genre, a consistent set of practices that could be called fantasy, seems to have been almost unthinkable until well into the last century.

One person who tried to think of fantasy as a unique form of discourse was Sir Herbert Read, a poet, critic, and art historian who produced (in 1935) one fantastic novel himself *(The Green Child)*. In his book on *English Prose Style* (first published in 1928 but revised in the late forties and reissued in 1952), Read devoted a chapter to what he called "Fantasy (Fancy)." Throughout this book Read was trying to organize prose styles into eight modes based upon Jung's classification of the four types of psychic function (thinking, feeling, sensation, and intuition) multiplied by the two types of psychic energy (extraversion and introversion). The kindest thing one can say about this effort is not that he was unequal to it, though he was, but that he often managed to ignore its difficulties and the inconsistencies in which he became enmeshed, and to present simply and directly the insights to which it led him. (One should also perhaps note in passing that attempts like this undoubtedly fueled Northrop Frye's far greater achievement in *Anatomy of Criticism*. For those interested in the matter, Read's scheme [Read 85] should be compared to Frye's theory of "continuous forms.")

Read complicated his work further by relying upon the Coleridgean distinction between imagination and fancy to separate a higher form called invention, about which he can find almost nothing to say, from the lower form called fantasy, about which he says some interesting things. Quoting Coleridge, Read observes that "fancy is concerned with fixities and definites. In other words it is an objective faculty. It does not deal with vague entities; it deals with things which are concrete, clearly perceptible, visibly defined" (126). This is excellent, applying equally well to the Grimm Brothers' "Little Briar-Rose" and Roger Zelazny's "A Rose for Ecclesiastes," but without the concept of invention, which he has given to "imagination," Read can go no further in his search for the pure essence of fantasy. When he comes to the point of naming a literary form in which fancy or fantasy embodies itself he can find only one: the fairy tale.

There is much to be learned from the impasse Read reached here. It is clear that he admired fantasy and knew something about it. He raised the truly interesting question of how the modern writer could generate a form of fantasy equivalent in power and beauty to folktales that have been shaped by many mouths over generations of transmission. And he lamented — in speaking of the *Thousand and One Nights* — that the "Western world does not seem to have conceived the necessity of fairy tales for grown-ups" (134). But the literary fantasy he most admired was Robert Southey's story of "The Three Bears," which, as he observes, "so perfectly conforms to the requirements of a folk tale that it has actually been adopted as such, and is everywhere and in almost every language reprinted and retold with little consciousness of the fact that it is a deliberate creation of an English writer of the early nineteenth century" (131).

Read had a powerful sense of the human need for fantasy. He suggested, quite astutely, that if writers could free themselves from the domination of Romantic modes of thinking, which allotted fancy (as opposed to imagination) only a subordinate role in cultural activity, then they might "turn to fantasy as a virgin soil, and give to English literature an entertainment comparable to the

Thousand and One Nights" (135). But he was prevented from reconceiving the possibilities of fantasy himself because his own thought remained, precisely, dominated by Romantic attitudes. Specifically, he insisted that fantasy always "dispenses with all logic and habit, and relies on the force of wonder alone," but he reserved what he called "imagination and invention" for other forms of discourse than the fantastic. Deprived of both logic and invention, fantasy could only be conceived of as a childish form: what Read himself called "fairy tales for adults." Trying to look ahead toward the development of a new fantastic fiction, Read, under the spell of the Romanticism he condemned, could do no more than gaze into the past. On a clear day he might have discerned George MacDonald looking toward and beyond him, for MacDonald could see in both directions.

In 1893, about a decade before he died, MacDonald wrote an introductory essay for an American edition of some of his fairy tales. The essay appeared in the same year in England in *A Dish of Orts*, there entitled "The Fantastic Imagination." In it MacDonald articulated what seem to me the most fundamental principles of fantasy. Let us listen to him: "The natural world has its laws, and no man must interfere with them in the way of presentment any more than in the way of use; but they themselves may suggest laws of other kinds, and man may, if he pleases, invent a little world of his own, with its own laws" (Boyer and Sahorski 15). This is the key to modern fantasy, indicating the point at which it breaks both with the traditional folktale and with the realistic novel. Fantasy offers us an invented world, with its own laws.

For their makers and their audiences, the folktales were mostly of this world, though attending to aspects of it normally hidden, dark, or mysterious. Only the development of positivistic science and its literary handmaiden, realism, made the folktales fantastic, because they made the actual world scientific and realistic. The discovery of folktales by sophisticated courtiers and scholars led almost instantly to the production of pseudo-folktales or fantasies grounded upon the peasant medievalism of the European folktales that we have come to know. The production of these "fairy tales," or *contes des fées,* as the French called them, has continued up to the present time. The sophisticated (or "sentimental," in Schiller's term) imitators of naive folk tellers found a world already made for them. They did not have to invent new worlds with new laws. But MacDonald, in his later years, had begun to frame the problems of fantasy in a new light. He was cautious about using his own fantasies as an example, because, as he put it, "my long past work in that kind might but poorly instance or illustrate my now matured judgment" (15). Thus the model he developed, however briefly, was a foreshadowing of a genre that had not yet established itself at the time when he wrote, and which Herbert Read could not describe even fifty years later: a genre based upon the fabrication of an invented world with its own laws. This is how MacDonald described such inventions:

> His world once invented, the highest law that
> comes next into play is, that there shall be harmony between the laws by which the new
> world has begun to exist; and in the process of
> his creation, the inventor must hold by those
> laws. The moment he forgets one of them, he
> makes the story, by his own postulates, in-

credible. To be able to live a moment in an imagined world, we must see the laws of its existence obeyed. Those broken, we fall out of it. The imagination in us, whose exercise is essential to the most temporary submission to the imagination of another, immediately, with the disappearance of law, ceases to act. (15)

What Macdonald has given us here is one of the keys to the craft of reading. It involves the "temporary submission" of "the imagination in us" to "the imagination of another." Both reader and writer are assumed to have imaginations, in this formulation, with the reader falling — but only temporarily — under the control of the writer's vision, after which the reader's critical faculty comes into play. But if the writer fails to maintain imaginative credibility, the spell is broken at once, and the reader falls from imagination into criticism. The writer must create a world for the reader to inhabit. But for MacDonald, a world is a world precisely because it has a system of laws: laws that harmonize with one another. This view is compatible, it should be noted, with both Victorian theology and positivistic science, which together formed the matrix from which the full-fledged genre of fantasy emerged. And it emerged side by side with another new genre that glorified the transformation of this world: science fiction. Moreover, though one can point to relatively pure examples of both science fiction and fantasy, for the most part the two genres were thoroughly entangled from the beginning.

In fact, for the first half of the twentieth century, it is fair to say that fantasy flourished only as a parasite on its more popular cousin, science fiction. Even such pure fantasists as Edgar Rice Burroughs and David Lindsay needed some of the trappings of science fiction to account for the other worlds that they wanted to construct. That Lindsay's extraordinary *Voyage to Arcturus* should need its frame of space travel is evidence of the weakness felt by those writers who wanted, in MacDonald's terms, to create little worlds of their own. Even C. S. Lewis, who despised the values that dominated the science fiction of his time, used its machinery in his space trilogy and did not publish his first Narnia volume until 1950.

The spectacle of L. Frank Baum (to whom I once dedicated a book) struggling to define his own enterprise — and to resist the call to become a major writer of fantasy — is as edifying as the biblical story of Jonah. Baum's attempt to define his project begins in the letter that appeared as an introduction to *The Wonderful Wizard of Oz* when it was first published in 1900.

> Folklore, legends, myths and fairy tales have followed childhood through the ages, for every healthy youngster has a wholesome and instinctive love for stories fantastic, marvelous and manifestly unreal. The winged fairies of Grimm and Andersen have brought more happiness to childish hearts than all other human creations.
>
> Yet the old-time fairy tale, having served for generations, may now be classed as "historical" in the children's library; for the time has come for a series of newer "wonder tales" in which the stereotyped genie, dwarf and fairy are eliminated, together with all the horrible and blood-curdling incidents devised by

their authors to point a fearsome moral to each tale. Modern education includes morality; therefore the modern child seeks only entertainment in its wonder-tales and gladly dispenses with all disagreeable incidents.

Having this thought in mind, the story of "The Wonderful Wizard of Oz" was written solely to please children of today. It aspires to being a modern fairy tale, in which the wonderment and joy are retained and the heartaches and nightmares are left out.

This introduction provides a plentiful supply of blossoms for those who like to boil roses. Let us put the kettle on and see what we can brew up. First of all, Baum quite clearly takes his point of departure from the traditional or "old-time" fairy tale, as he calls it. He is definitely writing modern fairy tales for children rather than for adults, and his books have remained children's classics, unlike the Alice books, for instance, which have a significant adult audience. Even so, Baum must find his own name for this new enterprise — more evidence that fantasy was not yet understood as a literary kind or genre. He called his "newer" mode of writing "wonder tales" — a term which did not stick. He also undertook to purge all the "horrible and blood-curdling incidents" from the "old-time" tales to produce a "modern fairy tale," with the "wonderment and joy" retained and the "heartaches and nightmares" left out. This proved easier to say than to do, of course, with the effort to be both dramatic and sanitary leading to such awkward episodes as the attack on Dorothy and her friends by wolves, who have been ordered by the Wicked Witch of the West to

"tear them into small pieces." In the event the Tin Woodman takes charge:

> "This is my fight," said the Woodman;
> "so get behind me and I will meet them as they
> come."
> He seized his axe, which he had made
> very sharp, and as the leader of the wolves
> came on the Tin Woodman swung his arm and
> chopped the wolf's head from its body, so that
> it immediately died. As soon as he could raise
> his axe another wolf came up, and he also fell
> under the sharp edge of the Tin Woodman's
> weapon. There were forty wolves, and forty
> times a wolf was killed; so that at last they all
> lay dead in a heap before the Woodman.
> (Baum 1900, 121)

Having wolves tear you into small pieces is neither nice
nor modern, but having them line up in a row of forty to
be decapitated by one person (a tin man with no super-
natural powers beyond life and durability) is simply im-
plausible — or unlawful, as MacDonald might have said.
It is a blemish and results in a momentary weakening of
the book's imaginative power — even over a child. (I
should add that I have been waiting more than sixty
years to make this criticism to somebody who might care
about it.)

The weakness of this episode might be contrasted
with such matters as the rusting of the Tin Woodman's
body or other instances where the logic of this new world
is developed in an inventive way. Even the matter of
eliminating the gruesome results in some truly fine mo-

ments, such as that of the Cowardly Lion's dinner. After his offer to kill a deer for the party is turned down on the grounds that it would make the Woodman weep and rust his jaws, the Lion takes care of himself: "But the lion went away into the forest and found his own supper, and no one ever knew what it was, for he didn't mention it" (58–59). Here Baum is able to let his lion be a lion but to keep the "horrible" or unpleasant aspects of this off stage.

In *The Wonderful Wizard of Oz*, of course, Baum was not a committed fantasist. Not only was he not committed to any ongoing enterprise called "The Oz Books," he was not even totally committed to his own invented world. Peter Beagle once remarked of another fantasist, "Tolkien believes in his world, and in all those who inhabit it" (Boyer and Sahorski 135). Baum did not feel this kind of commitment to his enterprise. If the Wizard is a humbug in that first book it is because Baum felt himself to be a humbug, too. The Emerald City itself is a kind of fraud, in which everything is green because seen through green spectacles. It is only halfway through the second book, *The Marvelous Land of Oz*, that the spectacles are dropped, with some characters wearing them and others not, as documented in John R. Neill's splendidly faithful illustrations to the ninth chapter. They are dropped in the midst of an invasion by General Jinjur's feminist army, of course, who loot the city of its emeralds by prying them up with their knitting needles, and in this confusion Baum switches from whimsy to fantasy. Henceforth, the Emerald City is really green.

Baum's resistance to continuing the Oz books is worthy of one of his own characters — the Reluctant Fantasist, perhaps. The comic traces of this reluctance can be found in the prefatory letters to each book after the first:

2. *The Marvelous Land of Oz.* "And now, although pleading guilty to a long delay, I have kept my promise in this book."

3. *Ozma of Oz.* "Indeed, could I do all my little friends ask, I should be obliged to write dozens of books to satisfy their demands."

4. *Dorothy and the Wizard of Oz.* "It's no use; no use at all. The children won't let me stop telling tales of the land of Oz. I know lots of other stories, and I hope to tell them, some time or another; but just now my loving tyrants won't allow me. They cry 'Oz — Oz! more about Oz, Mr. Baum!' and what can I do but obey their commands?"

5. *The Road to Oz.* "I thought I had written about Oz enough; but . . . have been fairly deluged with letters from children. . . . I have received some very remarkable news from The Land of Oz. . . . But it is such a long and exciting story that it must be saved for another book — and perhaps that book will be the last story that will ever be told about the Land of Oz."

6. *The Emerald City of Oz.* "There will be no lack of fairy-tale authors in the future, I am sure. My readers have told me what to do with Dorothy . . . and I have obeyed their mandates. . . . My readers know what they want and I try to please them. The result is very sat-

isfactory to the publishers, to me, and (I am quite sure) to the children. I hope, my dears, it will be long time before we are obliged to dissolve the partnership."

Like Jonah, Baum seems to have struggled against his fate, thinking each book — or the book after next — would be the last, until the sixth, in which he accepted fate, after being swallowed by the leviathan of success. There he speaks to his dear little readers of publishers and partnerships. The man who perhaps wanted no more than to be a humbug has become an institution, a factory which inputs letters of suggestion and turns out fantasies to order. It is a cautionary tale, funny and sad, a bittersweet American success story. The stories themselves, when read today by an adult, have moments of wit and charm, happily invented scenes and characters, but seem always to have been powered more by the wishes of their readers than by the vision of their writer, who never quite understood why his readers kept demanding, "Oz — Oz!"

If I complain, I complain as one who spent hours making maps of Oz — before they put them in the books, as they do now. Given where he was and who he was, Baum achieved something remarkable in those books. Among other things he made the great discovery that another world could be the basis for fictions that were not programmatically Utopian but simply pleasing in their combination of strangeness and familiarity. In doing this he made American fantasy possible for others, a situation hinted at in Samuel Delany's *Neveryóna:* "'Earlier today, Ergi, out on Black Avenue,' Madame Keyne called down, 'I saw a woman try to deliver some very interesting bricks to a slug-a-bed not yet up to receive his ship-ment. These bricks were yellow — not your usual red. I want you to find out everything you can about them: their manufacture, functionality, durability, cost, main-tenance — everything that contours their value, in any and every direction. See if they'd be good for paving. Then report back to me'" (Delany 137). "See if they'd be good for paving." I love that. Not only were they good for paving, those yellow bricks made a road that led someplace. But they couldn't lead there in Baum's day. He went as far as he could. He showed how a person could invent "a little world" which was not the medieval world of the folktales, but having made it, he never knew quite what to do with it.

I would contrast Baum with the creator of Narnia — a much more learned man — who knew only too well what to do with his created world. Both Baum and C. S. Lewis had the gift of invention. What Baum lacked was vision, a worldview that would support a world. Lewis suffered from the opposite problem: a vi-sion too thoroughly worked out, so that his fantastic world always threatens to become a mere vehicle for al-legorical meanings — and often succumbs. It was J. R. R. Tolkien who put it all together, who produced adult fan-tasy that has invention and vision, that is more memo-rable as itself than as the vehicle for any system of beliefs. He began with *The Hobbit* in 1937, of which he wrote to W. H. Auden, "It was unhappily really meant, as far as I was conscious, as a 'children's story,' and as I had not learned sense, then . . . it has some of the sillinesses of manner caught unthinkingly from the kind of stuff I had had served to me. . . . I deeply regret them. So do intelli-gent children" (Boyer and Sahorski 91). It is Tolkien, in his superb essay "On Fairy-Stories," who claims the name *fantasy* for the genre in which he himself aspired to work. He knew exactly what he was doing and knew what it should be called. *The Lord of the Rings* is the paradigm of fantasy in our time. If there is such a thing as science fantasy, we will be able to locate it by its resemblance to and difference from Tolkien's work.

I observed earlier that the genre we have learned to call science fiction has been entangled with its other, its antigenre, fantasy, from the beginning, as Herbert Read noted in his usual blundering but perceptive manner, saying of H. G. Wells that "he comes as near as any modern writer to a sense of pure fantasy. He errs, as in *The Time Machine*, by imparting to his fantasies a pseudoscientific logicality; it is as though having conceived one arbitrary fantasy he were compelled by the habits of his scientific training to work out the consequences of this fantasy" (Read 133–34). Here Read stumbled upon one of the better definitions of science fiction but treated the whole enterprise simply as fantasy gone wrong. Read himself has gone wrong here, of course, by following the pseudoscientific logicality of his own definitions, but I want to suggest that he is also, at a very profound level, right. He is right in seeing science fiction as a branch of fantasy.

Given the positivistic matrix that dominated thought in nineteenth-century England and America, continuing well into the twentieth century, works of fiction that sought to present alternate or secondary worlds were forced to align themselves according to the binary polarities offered by positivism: science or magic, extrapolation or escapism, this primary world transformed or a secondary world created: positivism itself or religion, the antagonist of science. Under this dispensation, many fantasists tried to don the mantle of science, and those who did not worked out of an essentially medieval religious position: not just Christianity, but a very Catholic version of it. This positioning essentially pitted the religion of science against the traditional religion of faith and revelation. The one looked forward toward the extension of human powers and happiness through scientific progress. The other mourned a lost universe permeated by ethical principle. Whenever the fictions of science turned into a struggle between good and evil, the text in question became a fantasy, whatever the furniture or machinery of its alternate world, for such notions as good and evil are grounded in the human past and in theology. There is no place for them in science.

If the expression "science fantasy" indicates anything beyond the desire of publishers to promote the books they have capitalized, it might simply designate most of what we have been calling science fiction for many decades. On the other hand, this term suggests that we might at last be sufficiently beyond positivism and beyond medieval religion to be confronted, finally, by a new form that has positioned itself beyond both the truth/fiction opposition of science and the good/evil opposition of religion. I am not sure that science fantasy is the best name for such a genre, but we may find that its very oxymoronic structure does indeed convey something important about this new and extremely interesting fictional development. Without pretending to have surveyed the entire field, I should like to conclude by noting that a work like Gene Wolfe's *Book of the New Sun* seems to me at least partly to have gone beyond the old religious and scientific oppositions, and that Samuel Delany's *Nevèrÿon, Tales of Nevèrÿon, Flight from Nevèrÿon, Nevèrÿóna,* and even his earlier *Triton* are exceptionally full and satisfying embodiments of an enterprise that might fairly be called science fantasy. And, of course, the most memorable works of Ursula K. Le Guin — books like *The Left Hand of Darkness* and *The Dispossessed* — belong to this category as well.

One cannot conclude a discussion on this topic in the year 2001, of course, without considering the interesting case of the Harry Potter books, which have dominated the best-seller lists for the past year or so. (As I write these words, the *New York Times Book Review* has just broken out a separate category of "Children's Chapter Books" to stop Harry from dominating the fiction list — and a separate category of illustrated children's books to stop Harry from cleaning up on the new children's list. I'm sure their advertisers were complaining. But the timing of this gesture was really blatant.) Simply as a fact of the marketplace, the Potter books command serious attention, but for our purposes, the interesting question is how this commercial matter is connected to the nature and quality of the texts themselves. These books did not become a commercial phenomenon by virtue of some clever advertising campaign. They made their way on their own, by "word of mouth," as we say, though the market will be busy for some time finding new ways to promote the books and milk the phenomenon for dollars, pounds, and other forms of wealth. They made their way, I should say, because they are very good books of their kind, and their kind is a kind we are deeply programmed to enjoy: science fantasy.

The Lord of the Rings is set in another world — a world with natural laws, to be sure, but clearly another world. The *Narnia* books begin in this world, but, once through the wardrobe, we are elsewhere and elsewhen, in a world of lawful fantasy. The Harry Potter books are significantly different from both of these. What J. K. Rowling has done with extraordinary skill is to bring fantasy into our actual world, so that the two sets of laws coexist on the same planet, or, to put it more precisely, so the laws of magic (which is entirely lawful in Rowling's formulation) work certain specific and limited exceptions to the laws of nature as understood by the Muggles, who live on an earth which (a) doesn't believe in magic and (b) thinks it is the devil's work. We need not worry too much about the contradiction between (a) and (b), since the Muggles, are both positivistic and superstitious, which strikes me as a very realistic picture of the world we live in and the people among whom we find ourselves. In this connection, it is worth noting that the British edition of the first Harry Potter novel was called *Harry Potter and the Philosopher's Stone* — which some American marketing genius changed into *"and the Sorcerer's Stone,"* convinced, no doubt, that sorcerers would sell a lot more books than philosophers. But the original title makes the important connection between the world of Harry Potter and the world of the alchemists who were the precursors of modern scientific thinkers.

Consider, for example, the following words from the English and American editions of the first Harry Potter volume. They are quoted from "an enormous old book":

- English: The ancient study of alchemy is concerned with making the Philosopher's Stone, a legendary substance with astonishing powers. The stone will transform any metal into pure gold . . .

- American: The ancient study of alchemy is concerned with making the Sorcerer's Stone, a legendary substance with astonishing powers. The stone will transform any metal into pure gold . . .

There is only one difference between the two passages, but that one different word makes the first passage true and the second one false. Or, to put it more circumspectly, that word *Philosopher* in the English edition connects the magic stone to the actual history of human thought in a way that the word *Sorcerer* in the American edition does not. Before the attempt to gain power over nature fragmented, in the seventeenth century, into the empirical sciences on the one hand and fruitless magic on the other, the study of alchemy was a kind of magical or fantastic science. It was the ancestor of modern chemistry and the physical sciences in general, which were called "natural philosophy" for some time before being given their modern names.

What is important here is the way that magic in the Harry Potter books exists alongside of science. It is as if, in this universe, when science and magic parted company, they did not turn into true and false natural philosophy but into two true and different visions of the world. As a character remarks in the fourth novel, Muggle science is a substitute for magic. My point is that J. K. Rowling is writing not fantasy but *science* fantasy, and she knows what she is doing. It is a pity her American publisher betrayed her in this instance by replacing the concept of the "philosopher's stone," and all its weight of history and meaning, with the empty expression "sorcerer's stone."

But let me try to be more precise about the nature of Rowling's achievement. One of her finest moves — perhaps the key to her achievement in these books — was to invent the Hogwarts School of Witchcraft and Wizardry. This move, so simple in conception, so complex in its working out, brings science and the fantastic together, making magic into a discipline, or rather a set of disciplines that can be contained in textbooks and a curriculum of courses like herbology, transfiguration, and history of magic ("the dullest subject"). Rowling, to be sure, has fun with the titles and authors of the required text books, as in *Magical Theory* by Adalbert Waffling. (Theory has a bad name everywhere!) And this very fun operates as a kind of alienation effect, breaking the fictional spell by reminding the reader that this is a fiction, a kind of hypothetical game, in which the crafty reader can share a joke with the author and then willingly suspend disbelief in the events narrated.

On the other hand, Rowling's world is absolutely lawful in George MacDonald's sense of the term. Her magic manages to be both magical, in the sense that it violates what we believe to be the physical laws of our universe, and lawful, in the sense that it maintains consistently its own laws. Nowhere is this more apparent than in the major instance of time travel in the third book, *Harry Potter and the Prisoner of Azkaban*. At a crucial moment, in mortal danger, Harry is rescued by a figure that he sees dimly but believes to resemble his dead father. Later, he and his schoolmate Hermione use magic to travel backward in time a few hours, with the injunction to make only one change in the world to which they return. When Harry comes to the moment when he was nearly killed, however, he intervenes to rescue his old self. When the brief temporal excursion is over, Harry realizes that the figure he took to be his father was in fact himself (which accounts for the resemblance) returning from the future. To my recollection, time travel has never been handled more effectively and persuasively than this. Rowling's craft led her to present the intervention from the future first and then to account for it by Harry's return to the recent past. Everything checks out. This sort of thing makes for a world so solid that Rowling can joke about it in the titles and authors of books and in other ways.

This is not the occasion for anything like a full discussion of her achievement. After all, as I write, only four of a projected seven books have been published. I wish to make only a few points, using her books as my example. First, science fantasy is alive and well, though, with the science part established, Rowling's world seems to grow more Manichean in each book. Second, the crafty reader will appreciate and respond to the craft of the writer — to the jokes that break the illusion and to the power of consistent imagination that restores and sustains it. Obviously, we need no generic concept to like these books. These roses do not require boiling. Their appeal has been enormous. But if we are to account for that appeal and appreciate the author's achievement in a full and lasting manner, it must certainly help to realize that she is carrying on a very viable tradition of science fantasy. Her books work because she has crafted her world with extreme care, and with an admirable amount of wit and joy.

Sacred Reading

A Fundamental Problem

"What does it mean? What does it mean? Not what does it mean to them, there, then. What does it mean to us, here, now. It's a facer, isn't it, boys. But we've all got to answer it."

W. H. Auden, "The Orators"

If genre is a consensus, a set of fore-understandings exterior to a text which enable us to follow that text, whether it is a sentence, a book, or a life, its existence explains why readers who share those fore-understandings rather exactly with the author of the text can read him more easily, but it also explains why we must read him differently.

Frank Kermode, *The Genesis of Secrecy*

We begin to learn how to read at home, perhaps, but the craft of reading is developed within larger institutional frameworks. In this country, at this time, that craft is taught mainly in churches and in schools. Throughout this book I have been concerned with how readers may learn the craft of reading, but I have also considered, from time to time, how it should — and should not — be taught. In this final essay I shall address more directly the question of the institutional sites from which ways of reading are advocated and in which they are taught. And in particular, I shall be advocating a change in the attitudes and practices of English departments toward reading. Put simply, I am going to urge that college and university English departments start taking reading seriously.

What would it mean to get serious about reading? What would it mean to *teach* reading seriously? It would mean a change — a fundamental change — in the way most English departments conceive of their enterprise. Most of us who inhabit English departments have thought of ourselves as teaching literature, or, more recently, culture — perceiving any improvement in our students' reading skills as a mere by-product of the grander enterprise. Teaching literature has been justified by the greatness of the great books themselves, which are believed to improve the minds, if not the souls, of those who read them. Teaching culture, on the other hand, has been justified on more political grounds, in terms of the development of political awareness in students or their social empowerment. I am sympathetic toward both of these acts of pedagogical faith — but I have become skeptical about the results. I also am aware that professors of English live in a hierarchical system, in which those who teach literature (or culture) look down upon those who teach writing. In such a system, we are inclined to resist describing our task as the teaching of reading, lest such a description bring us down to the level of the writing teachers, than which there is nothing lower. I say "we" by way of admitting that I teach literature and culture myself, and am thus caught up in the system I am describing — but I wear my "we" with a difference, because

I also teach writing and thus view the scene, at times, from the bottom up.

For the past few years I have been engaged in the admittedly quixotic enterprise of trying to overturn or undo this hierarchical structure, arguing that English departments should put rhetoric and the craft of reading at the center of their discipline, using all sorts of textual creatures, great and small, as specimens for analysis and models for imitation. But once we say "rhetoric," we seem to be talking about writing rather than reading. I would like to expand that familiar conception of rhetoric to include reading as a rhetorical activity, as a craft, or set of methods, for producing meanings from texts. In our current hierarchical system, however, teaching the craft of reading may be thought of as even more elementary than teaching writing, generating even less cultural capital for its practitioners, who thus occupy the very bottom of our academic totem pole. Yet it is not as if those at the top know nothing about the craft of reading. Many of our finest literary scholars and theoreticians have taken up questions of literary interpretation (or hermeneutics) in recent years, but so far as I know, the only people who have tried to connect our hermeneutical knowledge to a pedagogical practice are the lowly writing teachers, who have had little or nothing to lose by admitting that they were teaching reading as well, and the New Critics, who tried to raise the craft to an art. Currently, the literature people have been fighting for prestige with the cultural studies people, even starting their own professional organizations, and, of course, both of these combatants disdain the rhetoric people, who are thought to be doing something vaguely "remedial" that the mayor or the governor or somebody should put a stop to — and probably will, if you live in New York, anyway.

Well, I would like, quixotically, to end all this squabbling. And the magic lance that I will use to tilt at these fearsome windmills is nothing less than a concept of the craft of reading as the center of our disciplinary activities. If we want our students to share with us the pleasures of the texts we admire, if we want them to enjoy the textual power that comes with mastery of our language and our culture, we need only to take seriously our responsibility as teachers of reading, which we can do by simplifying and clarifying the ways of reading we have already learned to use in our studies of English literature and culture. What I want to propose is that we use this literary training not by expounding the Truth that is to be found in the Great Books but by teaching the craft of reading that we have learned by reading those books and other cultural texts.

I believe that a proper craft of reading — including what we learn from reading poems and other literary works — can and should be used as an instrument for the serious study of all kinds of textual objects. This is not — or need not be — a retreat into belletrism, for many reasons, the greatest of which is this: the literary craft of reading has a natural enemy that is at large in our world and working powerfully to change that world in ways that are hostile to literature as we know it and to our political freedoms, as we have known them. This enemy of crafty reading is fundamentalist literalism, of whatever kind, and wherever found. The fundamentalist way of reading is in conflict with the literary craft of reading all across our own culture and around the world as well.

The decision, a few years ago, of the Iranian government to rescind its death sentence on Salman Rushdie can stand as a clear example of how these two ways of reading conflict with each other — and what may be at stake in such conflicts. Rushdie's book asked for a crafty reading and received, in that case, a literalist one — backed up by a price on the author's head. Talk about taking reading seriously!

We can think of many other instances, I am sure, where these two ways of reading come into conflict. Attacks on *Huckleberry Finn* for its use of the word *nigger* reveal fundamentalism at work in a social rather than a religious context, but here, too, the basic opposition is between these two ways of reading. Often, as in the case of Rushdie, such conflicts are based upon the difference between religious and secular ways of understanding texts, because the fundamentalist way of reading aligns itself easily with organized religious practices, whereas the literary craft of reading contains an irreducible element of suspicion concerning dogma and orthodoxy. Most literary critics and theoreticians now find literature to be marked, if not by paradox and ambiguity, then by dialogic differences or hermeneutic incompleteness. For such interpreters, literature is not univocal. As Frank Kermode put it so eloquently in *The Genesis of Secrecy*, "all modern hermeneutics except those which are consciously reactionary" (123) reject the possibility of finding "a single truth at the heart of thing" (122). As long as what Kermode called the "modern" cultural situation prevails, the literary way of reading and the fundamentalist way — which is, of course, "consciously reactionary" — will always be at odds. I am personally sympathetic to Kermode's view of the matter, but I believe that he may have accepted too completely the modernist (or even poststructuralist) position on the absolute duplicity of texts. In the humbler craft of reading I am advocating, a primary assumption is that texts are intelligible, that we must assume an authorial intelligence behind them in order to "situate" any text. The crafty reader, however, should also refuse to push this assumption too far, should be ready to recognize inconsistencies and gaps, should recognize that the author is at best a realistic fiction of the reader rather than a being to whom the reader may have direct access by inspiration, prayer, or any other vehicle of communication.

This means that the craft of reading I am advocating incorporates a part of the fundamentalist position, is even sympathetic to the aims of fundamentalism, but finally rejects as impossible the idea of a fully "literal" reading of any text, for reasons I will soon explain in some detail. The craft of reading should be open and flexible with respect to the play of meanings in any text. This is quite compatible with New Critical teachings. But where the New Critics saw their method as moving poetry and its understanding out of the vulgar world of politics and mass communication, I see the craft of reading as having definite political implications that must bring it into conflict with certain other ways of interpreting texts. To illustrate this I am going to bring the literary craft of reading and the fundamentalist way of reading into direct conflict so as to illustrate as fully as I can just what is at stake in this difference.

Many people have thought that fundamentalist ways of thinking and reading would gradually lose their power as the world became progressively enlightened. Even Freud, who had many reasons to be skeptical about rationality, believed this. But I want to remind you that it has *not* happened. Just ask those science teachers who are being directed to present creationism alongside of evolution — if not instead of it — in some of our secondary schools. The appeals of fundamentalism are extremely powerful, and by no means confined to religion. Influential and extremely well-funded groups are attempting to read our Constitution and rewrite our laws in accordance with the letter of certain biblical texts — and to elect the legislators who will accomplish this for them. There is a serious struggle here, worthy of our fullest attention and demanding of our greatest powers.

We who live in English departments are by and large a docile group, who would rather avoid conflicts with the outside world than engage in them. We may be at one another's throats over the curriculum, or the leadership of our departments, or our parking places, but we have not liked to offend large and influential groups outside our academic walls. Nevertheless, if I am right about the essential and important opposition between the literary and the fundamentalist ways of reading, we shall have to risk doing so. We shall have to take a stand, and we shall have to bring both the sacred texts themselves and specific examples of fundamentalist reading into our classrooms to be examined. We need to do this because the literary craft of reading and fundamentalist ways of reading are linked in their very opposition. They are also linked in that they both take the problem of interpretation seriously; they both care a lot about what texts really mean. Crafty readings should allow more scope for textual pleasure, to be sure, but both approaches are very concerned about getting it right. What I am suggesting is that, in teaching the craft of reading, we should include examples of fundamentalist interpretation that will demonstrate just what is at stake in these two different ways of reading. "Teach the conflicts!" Gerald Graff has kept urging us, but he has meant mainly the conflicts within English departments rather than those larger struggles outside the boundaries of our academic groves. I am urging a somewhat different course, which is more exciting but also riskier. You must decide whether the stakes are worth the risks involved. But come, the game is afoot!

What does it mean to read a text in a *fundamentalist* way? Many people, including those who would take pride in being called fundamentalists, would describe fundamentalist reading as "literal" reading. So let us consider this word *literal* in a literary way. The *lit* in *literal* refers to letters, a letter being the smallest legible part of a word. But "literal" meaning is not the meaning of the letters, since meaning does not inhere in individual letters but in such larger verbal units as prefixes, suffixes, and whole words. The concept of a *literal* meaning, then, is itself an exaggeration, a metaphor, a paradox. Nevertheless, it is an expression of a desire to get at the truth of a text, which we must respect and share, even as we insist on the complexity — if not the impossibility — of such a task. The crafty reader, then, must acknowledge the seriousness of fundamentalist readings, while resisting and criticizing the zeal that often results in interpretive leaps to an unearned certainty of meaning, achieved by turning a deaf ear to the complexity of the texts themselves, their histories, and their present situations. On this occasion, I propose to recognize that seriousness by looking closely at an actual case of fundamentalist interpretation, in which the reading of certain texts has led to prescriptions for human behavior in the everyday lives of millions of people.

A case of fundamentalist reading which commanded media attention for a few weeks in the summer of 1998 can serve as our example. In June of that year the 8,500 delegates at a meeting of the Southern Baptist Convention voted overwhelmingly for an amendment to the Baptist faith that included the following controversial passage:

> The husband and wife are of equal worth before God, since both are created in God's image. The marriage relationship models the way God relates to his people. A husband is to love his wife as Christ loved the church. He has the God-given responsibility to provide for, to protect, and to lead his family. A wife is to submit herself graciously to the servant leadership of her husband even as the church willingly submits to the headship of Christ. She, being in the image of God as is her husband and thus equal to him, has the God-given responsibility to respect her husband and to serve as his helper in managing the household and nurturing the next generation. (Southern Baptist Convention)

This text will serve us well as an example of both the methods and the problems of fundamentalist reading. It is exemplary in a number of ways. First of all, it is itself a reading of other texts, based, as its authors insist, on certain passages in the letters of the Apostle Paul. I shall use it, then, not only as a text to be studied in itself but also as a text that illustrates a certain way of reading other texts. Let us begin, then, by looking at the way this text reads its Pauline pretexts. (I should note in passing that Genesis 1 and 2 are also important pretexts for this statement — and indeed are pretexts for Paul himself — that will have to be ignored in the present discussion.) R. Albert Mohler, president of the Southern Baptist Theological Seminary, says that submission of the wife to the husband is "not a modern idea" but "is clearly revealed in scripture" (quoted in Niebuhr). President Mohler's wife, Mary, who was on the committee that drafted the document, says, "The word 'submit' may be politically incorrect and unpopular, But it is a biblically correct word and that's what counts. . . . I submit to the leadership of my husband in our home, not because it is a command from Al Mohler, but because it is a command from almighty God to me as a Christian woman" (Internet source, now removed from Web).

What makes these readings of the biblical text "fundamentalist," as I am using the term, is, first of all, the decision to read the entire New Testament as the word of God, so that Paul's teachings must be treated as commands from the Almighty. This is a little different from reading those statements attributed directly to Jesus as the word of God. If one believes that Jesus is indeed the Son of God, and that he has been translated and quoted accurately, then the Sermon on the Mount, the parables, and other statements attributed to Jesus have a direct authority, a line of authentication that goes back to the Creator, making them, indeed, the word of God. (And some Bibles recognize this — by printing the words of Jesus in a different color, for instance.) But the letters of Paul are another matter. Leaving aside the question of who wrote them, about which whole books have been written, should his letters be given the same sort of authority as the teachings of the Lord he followed? If one answers this question in the affirmative, then *everything* Paul said must be taken as the word of God, which leads to other problems we shall be investigating later on. If, on the other hand, one answers in the negative, then one must separate, by an interpretive decision, those statements that have divine authority from those that have only the authority of the man, Paul, and, even further, those that may be read as simply the culture around Paul, speaking through his words.

What I have been calling the "fundamentalist" way of reading is based on the notion that the entire text is a divine utterance, with God speaking through Paul. But many of those who would call themselves fundamentalists do not adhere strictly to this principle. For this way of reading, David Scholer, a professor of New Testament at the Fuller Theological Seminary, has coined the phrase "selective literalism." Scholer points out that many of those who claim to be reading literally are in fact reading their own presuppositions into the text and ignoring things that do not match their own views. Southern Baptists, he points out, do not take literally Jesus' command that his followers wash one another's feet, though some other Baptists do (Steinfels). And there are other Pauline utterances, as we shall see, that these interpreters choose to ignore. As a student of the craft of reading, I would go further than Scholer, here, and argue that "selective literalism" is an inescapable feature of fundamentalist reading, because virtually every text presents internal difficulties that require a departure from the literal if a consistent reading is to be achieved. This is something that Paul himself seems to have understood quite well, since he shifts to an allegorical reading of the Old Testament whenever it suits his purposes.

The problem, as Frank Kermode has noted, is that a rigorous literalism inevitably encounters conflicts or problems—what Kermode has called "latent mysteries, intermittent radiances" (122)—and the resolution of these would lead the reader beyond fundamentalism to more complex interpretive methods. But fundamentalist reading normally rejects, denies, or conceals these difficulties, reducing meaning to what is already known or what is already allowed to be understood by the particular sect that claims authority over the text. To come back to the homely illustration with which we began this investigation, the line between what God said and what Al Mohler said may not be as easy to draw as Mary Mohler believes it to be. And in any case, someone called Paul stands between the two of them. To put this another way, confronted by any particular anomaly resulting from an attempt to read a text literally, the crafty reader will allow for an ambiguity or complexity that leaves the text open to further interpretation, while the fundamentalist reader will resort to selective literalism to force closure upon it.

This is, and I want to emphasize this, a matter of getting it right, of reading gaps and contradictions in the text precisely as gaps and contradictions, rather than silently filling those gaps with ideological cement—which is what usually happens. Textual fidelity, which should be a goal of the crafty reader, requires scrupulous attention to what is left out of the text and what is self-contradictory in the text, as well as to what is said clearly in the text—whether we want to get that message or not.

In a "situated" reading, we give "them, there, then" their due. With this in mind, let us return to the Southern Baptist Convention (SBC) and its reading of the New Testament.

The Southern Baptist Convention's statement on marriage, as I have indicated, is based on a reading of certain passages in Paul's Epistles, in particular Ephesians, chapter 5, and 1 Corinthians, chapter 11. I must apologize for the length of these quotations and ask you to bear with me in considering them. They must be quoted at length because the "selective literalism" of their interpreters becomes visible only when we can see what is being omitted that was present and what is being connected that was not so connected in the text:

Ephesians 5

21 and be subject to one another in fear of Christ.

22 Wives be subject to your husbands as to the Lord.

23 For the husband is the head of the wife, as Christ also is the head of the Church, He Himself being the Savior of the body.

24 But as the church is subject to Christ, so also the wives ought to be to their husbands in everything.

25 Husbands, love your wives, just as Christ also loved the church and gave himself up for her;

26 that he might sanctify her, having cleansed her by the washing of water with the word,

27 that he might present to Himself the
church in all her glory, having no spot or
wrinkle or any such thing; but that she
should be holy and blameless.

28 So husbands ought also to love their own
wives as their own bodies. He who loves
his wife loves himself;

29 for no one ever hated his own flesh, but
nourishes and cherishes it, just as Christ
does the church,

30 because we are members of His body.

1 Corinthians 11

3 But I want you to understand that Christ is
the head of every man, and the man is the
head of a woman, and God is the head of
Christ.

4 Every man who has something on his head
while praying or prophesying, disgraces
his head.

5 But every woman who has her head uncovered while praying or prophesying, disgraces her head; for she is one and the
same with she whose head is shaved.

6 For if a woman does not cover her head, let
her also have her hair cut off or her head
shaved, let her cover her head.

7 For a man ought not to have his head covered, since he is the image and glory of
God; but the woman is the glory of man.

8 For man does not originate from woman,
but woman from man;

9 for indeed man was not created for the
   woman's sake, but woman for the man's
   sake.
10 Therefore the woman ought to have a
   symbol of authority on her head, because
   of the angels.
11 However, in the Lord, neither is woman
   independent of man, nor is man independent of woman.
(New American Standard Bible, in Kohlenberger)

Insofar as the Southern Baptists' statement is a reading
of these passages (which they cite in their literature),
they are on strong ground with respect to the inequality
of men and women. They would seem to be on weaker
ground, however, with respect to their statement about
a wife "being in the image of God as is her husband
and thus equal to him," since Paul makes it quite clear in
1 Corinthians 11:3–11 that these are not equal images,
with respect to hair at least. And hair is important in this
case because it grows on heads, and the Pauline texts
give heads a special significance.

   The hair passage is a little cryptic, but the general
sense is clear. Men must appear before God, in praying
or prophesying, with no more covering on their heads
than their hair. Women may not; they must have addi-
tional covering, "because of the angels," or, as the Greek
original puts it, *dia tous angelous*, which might also be
translated "for the sake of the angels." If this passage
made clear and simple sense to Paul and the Corinthians,
it suggests a great cultural abyss between them and us,
since it is very difficult for modern readers to imagine

what those heavenly messengers had to do with hats. Would the angels have found the daughters of men too attractive if their hair were not concealed? Would the women's uncovered heads be wounded by the force of angelic inspiration? Might they have been impregnated like Mary, through the ear, by angelic words, if their heads were uncovered? This is an area in which interpretation must admit defeat, lacking the context that could make these words intelligible. Nevertheless, it is clear that an important inequality between men and women is being noted here by Paul, an inequality that is also presented through the metaphor of the body and the head in Ephesians 5:23–30.

The metaphor of the head and the body, which is very much a live metaphor in Paul's text, works against any notion of equality, since Paul teaches that the woman is equivalent to the body and the man to the head of the being that they make together, just as Christ is the head and the church is the body in the entity that they make, and, finally, Christ himself, having been incarnated — that is, given a body of flesh and bone through his human gestation and birth — has become a body of which God himself is the head. Thus the woman is to the man as the church is to Christ, and as Christ is to God. This is a hierarchical relation in which woman is the bottom, man above her, Christ above man, and God the Father at the top. This seems plain enough, even at a level of analysis that does not go deeply into interpretation. But there are other ways to read the Pauline text.

One well-informed reader of these texts, after noting certain elements of mutuality in the notion of marriage put forward by Paul, goes on to read Ephesians 5 in the following way:

The author of the Letter to the Ephesians sees no contradiction between an exhortation formulated in this way [that is, the way of mutuality] and the words: "Wives, be subject to your husbands, as to the Lord. For the husband is the head of the wife" (5:22–23). The author knows that this way of speaking, so profoundly rooted in the customs and religious tradition of the time, is to be understood and carried out in a new way: as a "*mutual subjection out of reverence for Christ*" (cf. Eph 5:21). This is especially true because the husband is called the "head" of the wife as Christ is the head of the Church; he is so in order to give "himself up for her" (Eph 5:25), and giving himself up for her means giving up even his own life. However, whereas in the relationship between Christ and the Church the subjection is only on the part of the Church, in the relationship between husband and wife the "subjection" is not one-sided but mutual.

In relation to the "old" this is evidently something "new": it is an innovation of the Gospel. We find various passages in which the apostolic writings express this innovation, even though they also communicate what is "old": what is rooted in the religious tradition of Israel, in its way of understanding and explaining the sacred texts, as for example the second chapter of the Book of Genesis.

This reader offers a theory of interpretation along with specific readings of the text. According to his theory, the interpreter must recognize that certain features are "old," "rooted in the religious tradition of Israel, in its way of understanding and explaining the sacred texts" — that is, part of the Jewish law — and that other features are "new," "an innovation of the Christian Gospel." This reader also insists that Paul himself, as the author of this text, is fully aware that the old Jewish law must be subordinated to the new Christian dispensation — and, indeed, there is plenty of textual evidence to support this interpretation. According to this way of reading, modern interpreters must follow the author's lead in interpreting his text and in acting upon its instructions: "The *author knows* [says this interpreter] that this way of speaking, so profoundly rooted in the customs and religious tradition of the time, is to be *understood and carried out* in a new way: as a 'mutual subjection out of reverence for Christ'" [italics added].

This reader, as you may have realized already, is Pope John Paul II, who offered his interpretation of Paul in his apostolic letter "On the Dignity and Vocation of Women" *(Mulieris Dignitatem)*. There are many interesting aspects of the pope's reading of the Pauline texts, but one of the obvious points of interest is the closeness of his reading to the Southern Baptist Convention's interpretation of the same texts. There is a certain amount of "selective literalism" in both readings. And selective literalism is a method of textual consumption that is opposed, in more than one way, to the craft of reading I am advocating here. I will go beyond this to say that students of literature should learn to recognize and be on their guard against selective literalism, because it is one of the most popular and powerful ways in which the reading public is misled. But let us look more closely at what the pope has done. (I should perhaps add, at this point, that I am pleased to have made my critique ecumenical in this fashion, since it was never my intention to single out any particular denomination for criticism or, as I have said, to indicate that selective literalism is used only in the service of religion. It is used whenever texts are considered "sacred," which happens in many fields of academic study and in the world of politics as well.)

Now before returning to the pope, I must pause briefly for some theoretical considerations. What I have been calling by the useful borrowed name "selective literalism" is a method of interpretation that has two parts — and the parts are not equal. If the search for a literal meaning is understood as a wish to close as fully as possible the gap between the presuppositions of the author and those of the reader, then an attempt to recover a literal meaning is a fundamental part of every act of interpretation. Umberto Eco has suggested that since it is so difficult to recover an achieved intention of the author of any text, we should seek what he calls the intention of the text itself (Eco 25). This has too much of the verbal shell game about it for me. We must seek an authorial intention, while recognizing that there are many reasons why we shall never close the gap that separates us from the author. The crafty reader must seek authorial intention knowing that what is found will never be exactly that. The truly fundamentalist reader must believe that the Author's intention is fully realized in the text — and that the reader may receive the amazing grace that will allow him (the gender is not accidental here) to register that intention. The process gets interesting when the reader's inspiration seems to lead toward a reading that is not literal. Once again, the Apostle Paul was well aware of this. He himself recommends reading not literally, according to "the letter," but according to "the spirit" — "for the letter (*gramma*) kills, but the spirit (*pneuma*) gives life" (2 Corinthians 3:6). But what if reading according to the spirit turns into selective literalism? *Selective* literalism is a problem because the adjective contradicts the noun. A reading that is only partly literal is simply not a literal reading, since *literal* is an absolute concept. But fundamentalist reading is always marked by shifts from the literal to the figurative — as a way of concealing conflicts. Paul himself occasionally makes shifts of just this sort in reading earlier biblical texts.

For these and other reasons, the problem faced by later interpreters of the Pauline text is a complicated one. The Southern Baptist Convention is inclined to describe the whole text as the "word of God." The pope refers to the "author" with a small "a," and in his reading seems willing to see this author as a man, located in time, trying to reconcile the old law with the new dispensation. If both approaches invest the text with a good deal of authority, the papal approach seems to allow more leeway for adjusting the interpretation — but only for adjusting it in a way that makes it compatible with an already established reading of the teachings of Jesus — which may be what Paul meant by reading according to the spirit. Interestingly enough, however, both the pope and the SBC make an identical interpretive move to soften the text's apparently hard line on the superiority of men over women. They both take Ephesians 5:21 — "and be subject to one another in the fear of Christ" — and connect it to the following discussion of marriage, which begins with the admonition, "Wives, be subject to your own husbands as to the Lord" (5:22). That is, they read 5:21

as referring to the marriage relationship specifically. This is a case where every editor of the Greek text and every translator (or group of translators) has had to make a decision that moves straight to the level of interpretation.

The (UBS) Greek text, if translated with maximum literalness and diagrammed to emphasize its structure, would look like this:

> 21 being subject to one another in fear of
> Christ,
> 22 the wives to their own husbands
> as to the lord,
> 23 for the husband is the head of the wife . . .

The first command, in verse 21, comes near the end of a long list of such prescriptions that seems, from the context, to be addressed to all the Ephesian faithful, regardless of their sex. Verse 22 preserves the syntax of commandment but is addressed directly to the wives, in language that is much like that used by Paul a few verses later in commanding slaves *(hoi douloi)* to obey their lords: the Greek word *kyrios* being used for both the husbands *(hos toi kyrioi)* and the slaves' masters *(kyrioi,* lords). (Ephesians 6:5–6, "Slaves, be obedient to those who are your masters according to the flesh, with fear and trembling, in the sincerity of your heart, as to Christ; not by way of eye-service, as men-pleasers, but as slaves of Christ, doing the will of God from the heart.") Paul, it appears, sees the marriage relationship as in certain respects analogous to slavery, with the wives subject to their husbands "in everything." He is also, it seems, thinking of slaves as sexual objects, concubines who may bear their lord's children but should not try (as "eye pleasers") to seduce him. The most telling feature of Paul's statement about the duties of wives, however, is that it is *not* followed by a reciprocal statement addressed to the husbands. That is, they are not told to be subject to their wives, though this is the spot where such an injunction ought to appear if that notion was indeed part of the intended message. This is one of those places where interpretation requires reading what is absent from a text as well as what is present — which is impossible in a literal reading. In this instance, husbands are not told to be subject to their wives, as one might expect, but, instead, to love them, to keep them clean and free of wrinkles, going so far as to love them as much as they love their own bodies. (The same instructions, for both wives and slaves, appear in almost the same words in Colossians 3:18–22.)

The Pauline text takes a similar attitude toward the possibility of women speaking in church or teaching. In the first Epistle to Timothy (chapter 2) Paul writes:

> 11 Let a woman quietly receive instruction
>   with entire submissiveness.
> 12 But I do not allow a woman to teach or ex-
>   ercise authority over a man, but to remain
>   quiet.

And in 1 Corinthians (chapter 14):

> 34 Let the women keep silent in the
>   churches; for they are not permitted to
>   speak, but let them subject themselves,
>   just as the Law also says.

35 And if they desire to learn anything, let
   them ask their own husbands at home; for
   it is improper for a woman to speak in
   church.

At the level of reading and interpretation, the fundamentalists, and the pope as well, have largely got Paul
right. And when Paul mentions that the law *also* says
this, he is indicating a point of agreement between the
Old Dispensation and the New Testament. (The SBC in
June 2000 voted to eliminate female pastors on the basis
of Paul's text.) The interpretive trick that both the pope
and the SBC performed, as I see it, lay not in insisting that
wives should submit, which is clearly Paul's teaching,
but in the way they took a statement about mutual subjection, which in context seems addressed to all members
of the congregation, male and female, and read it as if it
were about husbands and wives only, and specifically
about their behavior in the marriage relationship. This
was then used to demonstrate that because husbands
and wives are subject to each other, the statement that
wives must be subject to husbands is not significant of an
unequal relationship. As the pope put it, "Whereas in the
relationship between Christ and the Church the subjection is only on the part of the Church, in the relationship
between husband and wife the 'subjection' is not one-
sided but mutual." The pope is not a Jesuit, but he could
qualify. This is a nifty piece of casuistry. In this view, if I
may paraphrase Orwell, everyone is subject to everyone
else, but some are more subject than others. It is true,
however, that elsewhere in 1 Corinthians (chapter 7),
Paul indicates that although it is best for a man not to
touch a woman, it is nevertheless "better to marry than to

burn" (7:9), and that, in marriage, the man and woman
have obligations to each other:

> 3 Let the husband fulfill his duty to his wife,
>   and likewise also the wife to her husband.
> 4 The wife does not have authority over her
>   own body, but the husband does; and like-
>   wise also the husband does not have au-
>   thority over his own body but the wife
>   does.
> 5 Stop depriving one another, except by
>   agreement for a time that you may devote
>   yourselves to prayer, and come together
>   again lest Satan tempt you because of your
>   lack of self-control.

Mutual subjection is clearly advocated here — but with
respect to the body only, and specifically with respect to
sexual activity. Each is to satisfy the sexual needs of the
other. To interpret these lines as referring to anything
more than sex is clearly to stretch their "literal" meaning,
but the pope, just as clearly, wants to stretch every reference to mutual subjection as far as he possibly can.

The Southern Baptists are close to the pope here,
with their references to the "servant leadership" of the
husband. In more biblical language this might be called
the "slavish mastery" of the husband. It is, in any case,
literary language, a trope, an oxymoron, that requires a
literary reading. This reliance on a literary or rhetorical
figure, on the part of both these interpreters of the
Pauline texts, seems calculated to make those texts more
acceptable to a society in which women have come much
closer to political and economic equality with men, while

ensuring that there will always be a gap between the masterful slaves and the slavish masters — "because of the angels." As I interpret the Pauline texts, they cannot and should not be manipulated to make them acceptable in this way, because the inequalities are too deeply embedded in the text to be erased by anything short of blatantly selective literalism or massive infusions of a politically correct spirit over the letter. Furthermore, I believe that both the pope and the Southern Baptists fully understand the essential inequality of Paul's view of the two sexes and are trying to make it sound less stark than it is — while not really eliminating it. One of the Baptist leaders, for instance, was quoted in a Canadian journal as saying that "society today can't understand what Christians mean by submission. So this is really an in-house document, not a public statement. A different document would be needed to translate this into popular language" ("Faith," *Alberta Report*, July 27, 1998). In other words, the doctrine could be given a "spin" for popular consumption — but the phrase "servant leadership" has already set the text spinning.

Both the pope and the Southern Baptist Convention, it seems to me, bring criticism into the interpretive level of the process. That is, they have judged the Pauline text and found its teaching in need of revision. But they cannot admit this explicitly without opening the way to more profound criticisms of Paul's teaching and the authority of his text — upon which their own authority rests. Jesus, who was a punster and a spinner of parables, said that he would found his church on the rock called Peter, but Christianity actually rests upon the fluid pen of Paul. Paul himself was well aware of this, for in one extraordinary passage he tells the Corinthians (2

Corinthians 3:2–3) that they themselves are his letter, his epistle, "written not with ink but with the Spirit of the living God, not on tablets of stone, but on tablets of living hearts." Do the tablets of stone refer to the "rock" Peter as well as the tablets of Moses? An interesting literary question. But Paul's actual epistles might as well have been written in stone, for his words now endure as a sacred text that cannot be emended. To protect the authority of this text — which is essential to fundamentalist interpretation — one must insist on its eternal truth. This teaching was right for them, there, then, so it must be right for us, here, now.

The pope, as I have indicated, gives a bit of ground by explicitly historicizing the text and separating those statements in which the old law is inscribed from those inspired by the new dispensation. He can do this because he is less bound by fundamentalist literalism than the Southern Baptist Convention. But for both the pope and the Southern Baptist Convention, once the text has been interpreted properly, there can be no space for criticism. That is, the faithful cannot decide whether to live according to these precepts or not — and still remain faithful. They must submit to the power of the divine text — which means to the power of those who have themselves been authorized to interpret that text. And some Baptist congregations have left the Southern Baptist Convention precisely because they are critical of its interpretation of the Pauline text.

A crafty reading of the Pauline text has been implicit in my discussion of the fundamentalist readings, but perhaps, before concluding, I should pull those implications together and make my notion of such a reading more explicit. To read Paul's epistles in a literary way means attempting to situate the text and the writer of these letters in their own time, constructing, from the clues in the text, the persona of this writer, paying particular attention to his self-fashioning. As he tells his correspondents about his own sufferings for the cause, his imprisonment and beatings; as he returns again and again to the issue of sexual purity, stressing his own celibate status as a human ideal; as he addresses simple, personal remarks to this or that individual—he constructs a persona, a character, who is a version of the author of the text. A crafty reading would interrogate the reliability of that figure, and factor it into the reception of what he says. Such a reading would also take note of the gaps and the contradictions in the text. Where the pope says, "The author of the Letter to the Ephesians sees no contradiction . . ." the literary reader should be alert to the way that some contradiction detected by the pope was hidden or repressed by the author of the text the pope was reading. A crafty reader would recognize and even admire Paul's rhetorical power as a writer, and would follow his subtle shifts as a reader, as when he moves from literal to allegorical or spiritual modes of interpretation of earlier texts. The goal of this kind of reading would be to comprehend, as well as possible, Paul's presuppositions, to understand as fully as possible his prescriptions for human conduct, and, finally, having established to the best of our ability what this text meant to "them, there, then," to ask what it should mean to "us, here, now"—in order to determine its proper bearing on our own values and our conduct in the world.

To read the biblical text as literary, rather than sacred, would be to recognize its complexity and to open it to criticism, thus giving readers the freedom to accept or reject the values they have discovered there. It would also require, as Frank Kermode has eloquently put it, "some effort to divorce meaning from truth" (122). And this, of course, is just what fundamentalism cannot allow. For true believers, whether Christian or Muslim, Stalinist or Maoist, the tables of the law are written in stone, not in the human heart. They know the letter of the law already, and so need not read the text in a crafty, literary way. That is why they cherish the letter and mistrust the spirit of the text. Above all, they cannot accept this basic premise of modern literary study: that never in this life will we see the text face to face, but always as through a glass, darkly, so that we can only read and reread, to the best of our ability, unless we choose to cover our heads and bow to authority, "because of the angels."

Conclusion

A Crafty Reader

5. Norman Rockwell, *The Rail-Splitter.*

My epigraph is truly graphic, an image rather than a set of words. Let us read it. It shows a reader, reading, who is also a craftsman, holding a tool of his craft, an axe. His head is in the clouds, literally. His feet are on the ground. Behind his feet, in the distance, is a tiny cabin, possibly made of logs, with smoke coming out of its chimney. Closer to him is a fence made of rails split from logs. His coat is over his reading arm, as if he might have removed it to do some work with that axe before he picked up his book again. His garments are plain. He is intent upon his book. He is lanky, with a shock of black hair. If he were an actor, he might be Gary Cooper or Gregory Peck — or a character out of a Frank Capra film. He can certainly serve as a model of the crafty reader.

He is also quite recognizable. This image resembles photographs we have seen of him, though this version pushes his image in the direction of heroism, turns him into an icon. We know him, of course. His face is on Mount Rushmore. His stone body sits enthroned in Washington, D.C. This is the "rail-splitter," the crafty president who saw our nation through the bitter war between the southern and northern states, or between the Union and the states that tried and failed to secede from it. But this is Lincoln when he was a young farmer, studying law, hoping to rise in the world — and it is Lincoln idealized, a figure in our secular pantheon. In this image both the axe and the book represent crafts, agriculture and law, crafts that he mastered. This particular representation of him, as it happens, was made by Norman Rockwell, the great recorder — or constructor — of American hyperreality. And Lincoln looks like a giant in this image, like a figure out of our mythology, a Paul Bunyan, with his head actually displacing the clouds, and the cabin from which he emerged standing hardly taller than his boots. Rockwell has portrayed him in a style that echoes other American painters like Benton and Bellows. This is truly an American icon.

If he can stand, here, for the craftsman as reader, we should also recognize that he was himself an exceptionally crafty reader of his world and its written texts. If we were to look, for example, at the way he read our Constitution, as demonstrated in the famous address he gave at Cooper Union in New York City, we would find him there being as literal a reader of that document as the most conservative politician could wish — and crafty withal. We would find him accepting the gambit of those who would read the Constitution in the light of its originators' intentions, following out the voting records of the founding fathers to look for clues about their views with respect to the extension of human slavery to the western territories entering the Union. This is not the occasion to follow the crafty turns of his reading of this sacred text. It is enough to note that he set a standard for serious reading of an important document that should be a model for us all. And he did this, of course, without the benefit of years of formal schooling or the certification of academic degrees. Reading literally was one tool in a craft he had mastered. His own writing and speaking show us also how far he had progressed in expressive rhetoric. He can serve as one model, then, for all of us who wonder how and why we should read and write.

Each of us, however, must develop the craft of reading in a way that suits our needs and capabilities. There is no single method. T. S. Eliot once said that there was no method except to be very intelligent. I should prefer to say that, for those of us with middling gifts in the way of pure intelligence, serious attention to the craft of reading can take us quite far. We may acquire what is thought of as "intelligence" simply by using our minds as well as we can and giving them the equipment they need, which is to be found in the books and other texts around us. Reading is the route to intelligence, not the goal of it. It is proper attention to the craft of reading that will make the reader crafty.

Works Cited

Auden, W. H. *The English Auden: Poems, Essays, and Dramatic Writings, 1927–1939.* London: Faber, 1977.

Bair, Deirdre. *Anaïs Nin: A Biography.* New York: Penguin, 1995.

Barthes, Roland. *A Lover's Discourse: Fragments,* trans. Richard Howard. New York: Hill and Wang, 1978.

Baudrillard, Jean. *Simulations,* trans. Paul Foss, Paul Patton, and Philip Beitchman. New York: Semiotext(e), 1983.

Baum, L. Frank. *Dorothy and the Wizard of Oz.* Chicago: Reilly and Lee, c. 1908.

——. *The Emerald City of Oz.* Chicago: Reilly and Britton, c. 1910.

——. *The Marvelous Land of Oz.* Chicago: Reilly and Lee, c. 1904.

——. *Ozma of Oz.* Chicago: Reilly and Lee, c. 1902.

——. *The Road to Oz.* Chicago: Reilly and Britton, 1909.

——. *The Wonderful Wizard of Oz.* Chicago: G. M. Hill, 1900.

Beckett, Samuel. *Watt.* New York: Grove, 1959.

Benjamin, Walter. *Illuminations.* New York: Schocken, 1969.

Bennett, Arnold. *Literary Taste: How to Form It.* London: New Age, 1909.

Boyer, Robert H., and Kenneth J. Sahorski. *Fantasists on Fantasy.* New York: Avon, 1984.

Brittain, Vera. *Testament of Youth*. New York: Penguin, 1989.

Brooks, Cleanth, and Robert Penn Warren. *Understanding Poetry*. New York: Holt, 1st ed., 1938; 3d ed., 1960.

Bruccoli, Matthew. *Ross Macdonald*. New York: Harcourt, 1984.

Chandler, Raymond. *Killer in the Rain*. New York: Ballantine, 1980.

———. *Later Novels and Other Writings* (LOA 2). New York: Library of America, 1995.

———. *Stories and Early Novels* (LOA 1). New York: Library of America, 1995.

Chandler, Raymond, and Robert B. Parker. *Poodle Springs*. New York: Berkley, 1990.

Connolly, Cyril. *The Unquiet Grave*. New York: Viking, 1957.

Delany, Samuel. *Neveryóna*. New York: Bantam, 1983.

Deleuze, Gilles. *Proust and Signs*. New York: Braziller, 1972.

Eco, Umberto. *Interpretation and Overinterpretation*. Cambridge: Cambridge University Press, 1992.

Eder, Richard. "Patriotic Gore." *New York Times Book Review*, April 30, 2000.

Focillon, Henri. *The Life of Forms in Art*. New York: Zone, 1989.

Forster, E. M. *Aspects of the Novel*. New York: Harvest, 1963.

Frost, Robert. *"Come In" and Other Poems*. New York: Holt, 1943.

Glendinning, Victoria. *Rebecca West: A Life*. New York: Knopf, 1987.

Grimshaw, James A. *Cleanth Brooks and Robert Penn War-*

ren: A Literary Correspondence. Columbia: University of Missouri Press, 1998.

Guillén, Claudio. *Literature as System*. Princeton: Princeton University Press, 1971.

Hammett, Dashiell. *The Dain Curse*. New York: Vintage, 1989.

———. *The Glass Key*. New York: Vintage, 1989.

———. *The Maltese Falcon*. New York: Vintage, 1992.

———. *Red Harvest*. New York: Vintage, 1992.

———. *The Thin Man*. New York: Vintage, 1992.

Herrick, Robert. *Complete Poems in Three Volumes*. London: Chatto and Windus, 1876.

Isherwood, Christopher. *The Berlin Stories*. New York: New Directions, 1963 (contains two volumes, each numbered separately: *The Last of Mr. Norris* and *Goodbye to Berlin*).

John Paul II, Pope. Apostolic Letter *Mulieris Dignitatem: On the Dignity and Vocation of Women on the Occasion of the Marian Year*. http://www.vatican.va/ holy_father/john_paul_ii/apost_letters/docu- ments/hf_jp-ii_apl_15081988_mulieris-digni- tatem_en.html

Johnson, Samuel. *Selected Writings*, ed. Patrice Crutt- well. New York: Penguin, 1986.

Kermode, Frank. *The Genesis of Secrecy*. Cambridge: Har- vard University Press, 1979.

Kohlenberger, John R., gen. ed. *The Precise Parallel New Testament*. New York: Oxford University Press, 1995.

Lawrence, T. E. *Seven Pillars of Wisdom*. New York: An- chor, 1991.

Layman, Richard. *Shadow Man: The Life of Dashiell Ham- mett*. New York: Harcourt, 1981.

Léger, Fernand. *Functions of Painting*. New York: Viking, 1973.

Macdonald, Ross (Kenneth Millar). *The Galton Case*. New York: Vintage, 1996.

———. *The Moving Target*. New York: Vintage, 1998.

———. *Self-Portrait: Ceaselessly into the Past*. Santa Barbara: Capra, 1981.

———. *Sleeping Beauty*. New York: Bantam, 1980.

———. *The Underground Man*. New York: Vintage, 1996.

MacShane, Frank. *Selected Letters of Raymond Chandler*. New York: Delta, 1987.

Mew, Charlotte. *Collected Poems and Selected Prose*. Manchester, U.K.: Carcanet, 1997.

Millay, Edna St. Vincent. *Collected Poems*. New York: Harper, 1956.

Miller, Henry. *The Henry Miller Reader*, ed. Lawrence Durrell. New York: New Directions, 1959.

———. *Tropic of Cancer*. New York: Grove, 1980.

Nelson, Cary. *Repression and Recovery: Modern American Poetry and the Politics of Cultural Memory, 1910–1945*. Madison, University of Wisconsin Press.

Niebuhr, Gustav. "Southern Baptists Declare Wife Should 'Submit' to Her Husband." *New York Times*, June 10, 1998.

Nin, Anaïs. *The Diary of Anaïs Nin*, vol. 1, *1931–1934*. New York: Harcourt, 1994.

———. *Incest: The Unexpurgated Diary of Anaïs Nin, 1932-1934*. New York: Harcourt, 1992.

———. *The Journals of Anaïs Nin*, vol. 2. London: Quartet, 1974.

Orwell, George. *Homage to Catalonia*. New York: Harcourt, 1980.

Pound, Ezra. *Literary Essays of Ezra Pound*, ed. T. S. Eliot. New York: New Directions, 1968.

Priestley, Joseph. *A Course of Lectures on the Theory of Language and Universal Grammar, 1762*. London: Scolar, 1970.

Proust, Marcel. *Swann's Way*. New York: Random House, 1970.

Read, Herbert. *English Prose Style*. Boston: Beacon, 1963.

Riding, Alan. "Placing the Timeless Vermeer in the Chaos of His Time." *New York Times*, July 9, 2000.

Rockwell Packet. The Norman Rockwell Museum at Stockbridge. Stockbridge, Mass., 2000.

Rowling, J. K. *Harry Potter and the Chamber of Secrets*. London: Bloomsbury, 1998.

―――. *Harry Potter and the Goblet of Fire*. New York: Scholastic, 2000.

―――. *Harry Potter and the Philosopher's Stone*. London: Bloomsbury, 1997.

―――. *Harry Potter and the Prisoner of Azkaban*. New York: Scholastic, 1999.

―――. *Harry Potter and the Sorcerer's Stone*. New York: Scholastic, 1999.

Sassoon, Siegfried. *The Weald of Youth*. New York: Viking, 1942.

Scholes, Robert. *The Rise and Fall of English*. New Haven: Yale University Press, 1998.

―――. *Structuralism in Literature: An Introduction*. New Haven: Yale University Press, 1974.

Scholes, Robert, Nancy R. Comley, and Gregory L. Ulmer. *Text Book: New and Improved*. New York: St. Martin's, 1995.

Scholes, Robert, and Robert Kellogg. *The Nature of Narrative*. New York: Oxford University Press, 1966.

Smith, Stevie. *Me, Again*. New York: Vintage, 1983.

Southern Baptist Convention. Amendment to the Baptist Faith, 1998. http://www.cbmw.org/html/baptist_statement.html

Stallman, Robert W., ed. *Critiques and Essays in Criticism*. New York: Ronald, 1949.

Stein, Gertrude. *The Autobiography of Alice B. Toklas*. New York: Vintage, 1990.

Steinfels, Peter. "Beliefs." *New York Times*, June 13, 1998.

Toklas, Alice B. *What Is Remembered*. San Fransico: North Point, 1985.

Trent, Lucia, and Ralph Cheney, eds. *America Arraigned!* New York: Dean, 1928.

Van Dine, S. S. (Willard Huntington Wright). *The Benson Murder Case*. New York: Scribner's, 1928.

———. *Philo Vance Murder Cases*. New York: Scribner's, 1936.

Vinh, Alphonse, ed. *Cleanth Brooks and Allen Tate: Collected Letters, 1933–1976*. Columbia: University of Missouri Press, 1998.

Wallace, Robert, and James G. Taaffe, eds. *Poems on Poetry*. New York: Dutton, 1965.

West, Rebecca. *Black Lamb and Grey Falcon*. New York: Penguin, 1994.

Wimsatt, W. K., Jr. *The Verbal Icon*. Lexington: University of Kentucky Press, 1954.

Woolf, Virginia. *The Diary of Virginia Woolf*, ed. in 5 vols. by Anne Olivier Bell, assisted by Andrew McNeillie. New York: Harvest, 1978–84.

Yeats, William Butler. *Collected Poems*. New York: Macmillan, 1959.

Index